JUST FOR FUN

No 3829
31-7-35
RayNeon

LUNA PARK
JUST FOR FUN

SAM MARSHALL

LUNA PARK RESERVE TRUST

Cover, 1960s face.
Back cover, cartoon by Jeremy for Re-opening 1995.

p. 1, restored carousel.
p. 2, blueprint of neon lights for 1935 face.
p. 3, Coney Island band mural by Arthur Barton.

This page left: 1960s face; *centre:* clown in front of the Bazooka face and Rock-o-Plane; *right:* 1973 face.

First published in 1995 by the
Luna Park Reserve Trust

Edited, designed and produced for the Luna Park Reserve Trust by Chapter & Verse, 18 Mitchell Street, McMahons Point NSW 2060

Edited by Carol Dettmann
Designed by John Witzig

National Library of Australia
Cataloguing-in-Publication data:

Marshall, Sam.
Luna Park just for fun.

Bibliography.
Includes index.
ISBN 0 646 21621 X.

1. Amusement parks - New South Wales - Sydney - History. 2. Luna Park (Sydney, N.S.W.) - History. I. Luna Park Reserve Trust. II. Title.

791.0689441

Printed by Star Printery Pty Ltd
Erskineville NSW

The illustrations in this book have been reproduced courtesy of many sources. A list appears on page 9.

CONTENTS

Arthur Barton ski scene and face on slides in Coney Island.

PREFACE

Tumble Bug.

This book celebrates sixty years of fun provided by Luna Park. There were various sources of inspiration for this book – the many people who had been to Luna Park and who had unusually fond memories; the very special breed of devoted people who worked at this amusement park which had been allowed to all but disappear and which few people remembered in its entirety; the existence of Ted Hopkins' superb photographic record; and the salvation of Luna Park by the group of determined citizens from all backgrounds, ages and professions who came together to fight a battle for the children of the future.

I wanted this book to be told by the people who worked at Luna Park, the general public who had fun at Luna Park and the people who fought to save Luna Park. They all get their opportunity to speak in this book.

Popular culture is not often seen as worthy of historical research. Documented information on Luna Park is very limited. The Local Studies Section of North Sydney's Stanton Library holds the most extensive collection of records on Luna Park including news clippings, photographs and original artefacts. I cast a wide net for information, conducting oral history interviews with as many past staff members as possible. I contacted the general public through all forms of news media to ask for their personal reminiscences. I welcome further information, photographs and especially personal reminiscences.

The text, photographs and anecdotes of this book are intended to be read together. Facts are presented in the text; the photographs animate and legitimate the text; the anecdotes bring all this to life. People who have

either spent most of their working lives at Luna Park or are publicly known are fully described. Anecdotes from the general public are attributed by christian names and suburb.

I am indebted to many peoples' generous provision of both time and material: in particular Ted Hopkins whose face would often become animated while discussing some technicality as he recalled some special amusing incident. Most of the photographs in this book were taken by Ted, a highly skilled amateur photographer. I thank his daughter, Margaret House, for kindly allowing the use of these images.

My final debt of thanks is to Martin Sharp. Without Martin there would be no photographs nor memorabilia and certainly no Luna Park. His foresight, wisdom and artistic skills have been a guiding light to me and those who fought to see Luna Park retained and put it all back together again.

Sam Marshall
Sydney
November 1994

Top: Entrance to Davy Jones Locker; *above right:* Bazooka face; *right:* U Drive.

Above: Tiny Tim
Opposite page: Sam Marshall.

ACKNOWLEDGEMENTS

The illustrations in this book have been reproduced courtesy of the following sources. Every effort has been made to trace copyright holders and the author and publisher apologise for any unintended infringements.

Andrew, Jeremy, p. 139 top as published in *The Sydney Morning Herald, back cover.*
Anonymous, p. 79 right.
Australian Broadcasting Corporation, p. 135.
Australia Post, p. 137 bottom left.
Barker, Michael, pp. 3, 5, 73 bottom.
Brown, Warren, p. 132 bottom left
Buffalo & Erie Historical Society (Pan American Exposition Collection), p. 31.
Buggy, Mary, p. 12.
Channel 9, p. 136.
Coopes, Jenny, p. 136 bottom.
Coulter, R.C.G. (courtesy Road & Transport Authority, from the Richard Raxworthy Collection), p. 55 top.
Daily Telegraph Mirror, pp. 81 top, 105, 113 bottom, 137 bottom right.
Day, Kathy, p. 123 bottom right.

Fairfax Photo Library, pp. 9 (Pearce), 92 right (Burke), 104, 131 top right (O'Grady), 135 bottom
Fink, Leon and Spatt, Nathan, pp. 107 top left, 117, 122, 123 top & bottom left, 128 top.
Foy, Rex, p. 16.
Friends of Luna Park, pp. 118, 119.
Halls, G., p. 45.
Harrison, Wall, pp. 100 right, 102 top left.
Hartwick, Andrew, p. 113 top.
Hopkins, Ted, (all reproduced with the kind permission of Margaret House): pp. 4 left and centre, 6, 7 top right and bottom, 8, 10, 12, 13 (courtesy Stanton Library), 14, 17, 18, 19, 20, 22, 23, 24, 25, 27, 53, 57, 58 right, 59, 60, 61, 62 (courtesy Stanton Library), 64, 65, 68, 69, 70, 71, 72 top, 73 top, 74, 75, 76, 77, 78, 79 top left, 80 (top right courtesy Stanton Library), (bottom right courtesy Lynette Wayling), 81 bottom, 82, 83 top, 84, 85 top, 86, 87, 88 right, 89, 90, 92 left, 93, 94 (courtesy Stanton Library), 95, 96, 97 bottom right, 98 (left courtesy Stanton Library), 99 right, 100 left, 101 top left and right, 102 top right, bottom left and right, 103 top left and bottom right, 106, 126 top, 127 top left, 145.
Howlett, Caroline Foulkes, p. 79 bottom.
Hrusousky, George, for the Luna Park Reserve Trust, p. 140 top.
Kimberley Clark Collection, p. 42 top.
Kingston, Peter, p. 117 bottom.
Larkin Aircraft Supply Co., p. 40 top.
Luna Park Milsons Point, pp. 83 bottom (courtesy June Baldwin), 85 bottom, 91 bottom, 103 top right, 110 bottom.
Luna Park St Kilda, pp. 37 bottom, 38, 39, 40 bottom, 42 bottom, 43, 48, 50.
McConnell, Smith & Johnson, p. 139 bottom,
Maher, Ken & Partners, p. 140 top.
Marshall, Sam, pp. 1, 121 top, 123 bottom left, 126 top, 130 right and left, 131 top left, 133, 134, 135 top, 140 bottom, 142, 148, 150.
Martin, Matthew, p. 138 top.
Mombassa, Reg, pp. 146, 147 top right.
Mosman Daily, p. 110.
Museum of New York City, pp. 29, 33 (Photograph by Adolph Witteman, The Leonard Hassam Bogart Collection).
Nicholson, Michael, p. 138 bottom.
NSW Archives Office, p. 54 top.
NSW State Rail Authority, p. 54 bottom.

Postcards, pp. 34, 36.
Sharp, Martin (taken by Michael Barker & William Yang), cover, pp. 2, 4 right, 7 top left, 8, 101 bottom left, 107 top right and bottom right, 108, 109, 114, 115, 116, 120, 121 bottom, 124, 125, 127 bottom left and right, 128 bottom, 129, 144.
Smith, D. Damian, p. 51.
State Library of New South Wales (Government Printing Office Collection), pp. 55 bottom
State Library of South Australia (Mortlock Library), pp. 46 (SSL:M:B7422), 48 top (SSL:M:B12707), 49 (SSL:M:B7478).
Stuart Bros, p. 56
Weight, Greg, pp. 91 bottom, 112 bottom, 140 top, 143, 147 bottom.
Whitney Bros, p. 37 top
Yang, William, p. 111
Zanetti, Paul. p. 132 top right cartoon courtesy of Paul Zanetti.
The author gratefully acknowledges photographs lent by: Kathy Day, Godden Mackay, Tom Ingram, Luna Park Reserve Trust, Luna Park St Kilda, Tony Maloney, Dick Pearce, Martin Sharp, Stanton Library Local Studies Section.

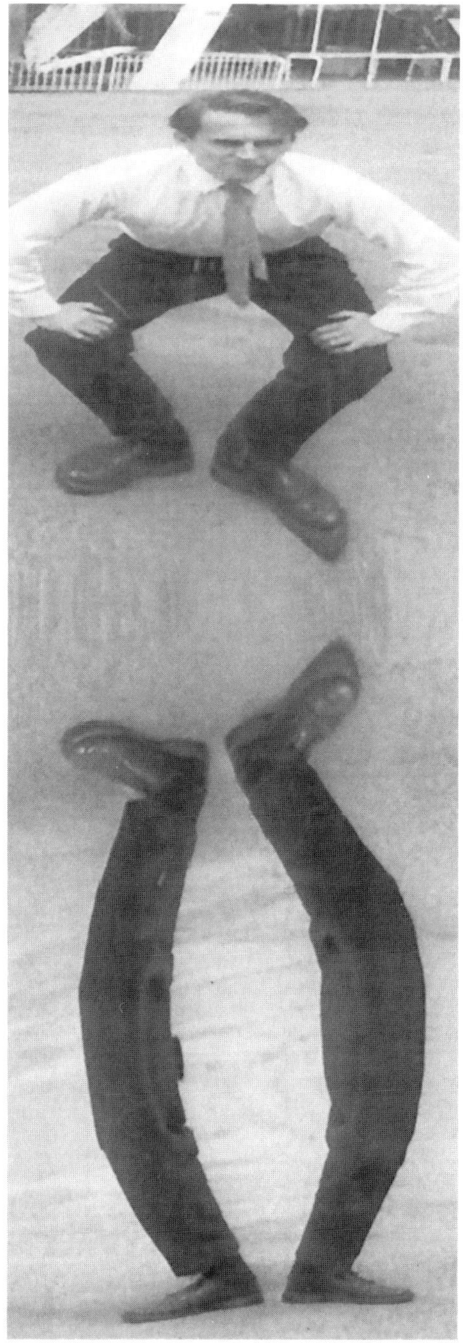

Alfred Street sign, c. 1935.

OPEN

Weeks of delirious anticipation were over. We'd gone without for weeks, pleaded for extra pocket money, lost sleep and dreamt of the delights to come.

Now we are swarming out of Milsons Point Station, down Alfred Street where a gigantic sign proclaims ENTRANCE TO LUNA PARK in brilliant neon. Its size is a hint of what is to come.

Down the hill, scale shifts from the everyday to the massive. The ground drops beneath the approaches to the Harbour Bridge, revealing Egyptian-scaled space. Ahead, the black oily expanse of harbour is dashed with ferries. Beyond lies the scheming metropolis. The pack veers to the right to be confronted with disbelief – a face large enough to take on all that it faces.

Our mates who have taken the first ride in the *Kuttabul* across the harbour under the huge Bridge now jostle with us in a restless queue as long as a football field.

Ahead is uncertainty. The 50 times life-size face with coloured neon pupils that scan its prey from side to side and raise flickering eyebrows and corona to heighten the expression of wonder, threatens to gobble us up. We are about to find out.

The outbreak of war in Abyssinia today and the spiral of the world to war mean nothing to us. It is 4 October 1935 – Eight Hour Day long weekend. Sydneysiders are seconds away from getting their hands on their own Luna Park and nothing else worries us.

CHARGE! 8.00 p.m. The gates are open.

Like lemmings we spill into the body of fun. Inside is like a kids' version of the David Jones' January clearance sale – people running every which

Waiting at Circular Quay for the ferry to Luna Park.

Eight, maybe seven I was, a kid from the bush in short pants with a basin cut and a hand-knitted sleeveless jumper two sizes too small, a junior hick suddenly exposed to the Big City. Not to mention the Big Dipper. Manly was amazing, ditto Bondi. And the city was pretty amazing too. But there was nothing quite like Luna Park for sheer magic. Childhood memories of this wondrous, sometimes tacky place are things that unite entire generations of Australians.

– Leo Schofield

All that time waiting made it all the more terrific.

– anon.

Closing my eyes as hard as I could didn't make it any less scary.

– Mark

way for the ride of their choice, not really knowing what they are letting themselves in for.

We've survived the gaping mouth, but will we be lost forever in the dark passages of Noah's Ark, be flung into the harbour from the Whip, be able to drive on a road again after the Dodgems, come off on a screaming curve while admiring the city lights on the Big Dipper or want to return home after the River Caves? More importantly, will we ever want to leave this sanctuary from reality? We don't care as we sprint down the Midway, past giant insects, a French Chateau, rocking skeletons, a revolving windmill, a gawking pelican – all huge, all out of context and scale. All ours.

What first? There's no question – the Big Dipper – the sorter of men from mice. A carload of thundering screams roars past in the opposite direction as the guard rail drops down into our laps. No means of escape now. We roll out of the station past a well-manicured garden among the white timber supports. A sign at the base of the initial steep incline warns Do Not Stand Up. Our car bites into the chain to jerk us away from the comfort of the crowd. We rise from the bowels of the Park through the white meccano sticks that we place our trust in. Again we are being plucked from reality, this time raised up above the screams, whirling coloured lights and swarming ants below. Clack, clack, clack, clack, clack – each notch closer to our greatest fears. Below the frenzied Midway becomes clear – an artery feeding the rides. Ahead the track disappears into the night sky. At the top a split second of deception – quiet solitude with the best view of Sydney. Jumpin' crickets, there's no track ahead! Gravity takes up the slack. Our father who art in heaven, hallowed be thy...have we done the right...too late...hang on.

As we roll over the precipice, 24 of us simultaneously breathe in. The previously giggling gerties in the seat behind us test our eardrums. Others test their impersonations of the mouths of the laughing clowns. I test my grip. What are the lunatics in front doing with their hands up in the air? Have their white knuckles already crushed the guard rail, or have they completely lost their marbles and now, in this moment of psychic numbing, are they raising their hands in prayer to the religion of thrills.

The burden of gravity on our bodies eases off as the slide down the first dip speeds up. The bloke in front's hat blows off. Forget it. At the dip of the dip, the opposite – our bums are driven down into the red leather-upholstered seats. Our guts follow.

Momentum takes us to the top of the dip. We travel slowly now around the curve of the figure-eight track. A moment's contemplation as we take in the breathtaking view (in case you need something else that was breathtaking) and prepare for more of what we've only just survived. Back down, this time under where we had just come. Will we lose our heads on the track over? Everyone ducks down to the level of the safety bar. No time to take risks and check whether heads are still on as the steep banked corner poses the question what on earth is holding this thing on the tracks. White posts race past along with images of wheels coming loose and tracks

Luna Park 1935.

Above: Goofy House and Noah's Ark, c. 1935;
right: Heydey, c. 1935.

breaking free and a blue-overalled maintenance man forgetting the split pin that holds on the undertrack safety wheel. Our lives are in his hands.

The remainder of the journey winds through the now dense white skeleton of the Dipper, brushing the cliff face and other screaming cars. There is little time to notice the shed-like backs of the Ghost Train and River Caves built from what appears to be a pile of driftwood. After several camel-backs and a final curve, light appears at the end of the straight where men in red coats prepare to pack the next bunch of masochists into our car that now has no chance of stopping in time. One of them pulls back heavily on the big dumb-looking lever that lifts a long slab of timber and us off the track. Again we all simultaneously take in a breath on dead stop. The attendant crowbars fingers off the guard rail. Jellied knees support frail bodies with hair in the post-hurricane style and faces alternating between exhilaration and terror. Some remain on the car while others desperately search for a suitable place to deposit what only minutes earlier had tasted wickedly delicious.

More. What next?

Bugger these queues, let's head back to the entrance to have a look at what is inside that huge boat that was rocking – was it rocking?

On the way, we each pick up a bucket of salty hot chips under the Old Windmill with blades revolving despite the windless night.

Yes, Noah's Ark with Noah and the heads of the animals poking out of the Ark's cabin is rocking either on choppy mountainous high seas or on top of Mt Ararat. There's hardly a queue, let's give it a go.

As we shuffle into this Biblical scene made concrete (or made papier-mâché), we notice on one side a huge silver insect, a tumble bug, whatever that is – a long lost species of arthropod perhaps. On the other side is a man's head complete with boater hat the size of a house. It is a house, the Goofy House. We'll have to investigate that later as we pay our 3d and now feel our way through the dark gusty maze-like passages. A miniature train charges around a room on a shelf near the ceiling. A spongy, matted floor falls away from under us and rises up again. Then our feet take on a mad dancing step as they endeavour to negotiate horizontal rollers on the floor. Handrails either side prevent us from ending up arse over tit. There is a spot where only girls wearing skirts giggled.

A window lights up to reveal a woman's head then fades away. Another box has the caption WHAT THE BUTLER SAW and inside is a piece of toast. We all look at each other. The next box unites us in that universally guaranteed provoker of laughter – mention of poo and wee. The caption says AN OLD TIME MOVIE and inside is a bottle of Epsom Salts. We move cautiously over some normal floorboards then a floor that rattles and up an incline to the entry of the Ark itself. We march in two by two. Jazz boards (slabs of timber moving backwards and forwards past each other) have to be negotiated as a gangplank to the boat. The Ark rocks gently. We are on the high seas. Inside the cabin is yet another surprise: Noah is not there but rather peep shows and mutascopes – gulp, this is what lurks under women's dresses.

I remember 5 consecutive rides on the Big Dipper until we were sick! Great fun.
– D. Galloway

I rode the Big Dipper 13 times without getting off.
– Michael, Marrickville.

My friend and I once rode the Big Dipper 15 times.
– Jane, Wollstonecraft

On each return visit to Luna Park, the tension and fear would build again as the wood against steel rattle grew louder as the ferry drew closer to undoubtedly the best place I ever went to as a kid.
– Anthony, Maroubra

There was a fella in there with a feather. He used to tickle all the girls' legs.
– Dick, Camden

Neon illuminated face.

We recently celebrated out Golden Wedding. We met on a blind date at Luna Park.
– Winifred, Taree

My brother, sister and I are all "Luna Park" babies. Mum and Dad worked at Luna Park and met over the Fairy Floss counter.
– Kathleen, Killara West

Down a deep well is a living mermaid – under water. She is alive, she's looking up at us. Outside is a commanding view of the Park.

Get a load of that. Ahead of us on the way out, girls involuntarily give us an real viewing of what the mutascopes had flickered – suspender-supported-stocking-clad legs. To us, the gusty air from the floor merely cools our knobbly knees and balloons out our baggy shorts. Older blokes have their hats blown off. The exit poses a choice – sissies walk down a ramp; we take the slide.

Outside, the girls ahead swing hard left not to be followed into the women's toilets. We go the other way to the Goofy House next door. Entry is not through a door but again a mouth whose adjacent eyes are striped sunshades under a straw boater hat as a roof.

Inside disbelief. An attendant in a tuxedo takes us up a flight of stairs to a woman's head with no body, only a frilly collar, whose chin is balanced on a sword. "This is the Magic Sword Illusion. This young lady had her head severed from her body but she can still smile and speak," and she speaks: "Hello, how are you?" Some smart alec comments "Look, mum, no hands."

Next a skeleton turns into a beautiful woman. Further on there is a full-size, living girl's head in a miniature bed on a glass table. A barrier prevents questioning eyes from finding strings, mirrors, whatever.

Then as we look at a sculpted head of a woman, the attendant announces the Sculptor's Dream: a story about a sculptor who was sculpting this head and shoulders and who fell asleep, dreaming that the head belonged to a beautiful woman. With that the sculpture turns into a beautiful woman before our eyes. "You're alive, aren't you?" the attendant asks and she replies "Yes". Cripes. Then we are told that the sculptor was in love and everything with her but when he woke up, she was a skeleton – which appears in front of us. Someone in the room squeals.

We duck under the legs of a sailor into a room that has 35,000 images of ourselves. Time for a quick jig and a good laugh. Past mirrors and hooting horns, we enter a room where water travels up hill and falls into a bucket, a flame burns at an angle and timber balls rattle uphill around the walls. A steel ball spins on a plate. I pick the ball up. There are no strings. When I put it down it spins again. There is a seat that takes a great effort to get up from. Something is out of whack.

Outside is even more sex education: a beautiful young girl in a woollen swimming costume with a coronet of pink geraniums sits in the mouth of a sea monster. A big crowd watches men hurl balls at a target in its eye. The "dong" of a bell indicates their success as she is gobbled up – dunked into a tank of water. A proud dunker, having proved his manhood, collects a box of Hoadley's chocolates. He promptly hands them back to the attendant saying to the waterlogged dunkee, "Here, these are for you, love." She is Sweetie and the game is Let's Duk Sweetie.

The saltiness of the earlier chips makes us easy prey for the sweet smell of vanilla wafting out of the French Chateau. Some order pink fairy floss in

Most blokes had their first perve of a woman at Luna Park.

– Peter, Burwood

Let's Duk Sweetie (Pat Noble) with Fred Switeley (left) and the Luna Park Band.

Above: Central skeleton on the Ghost Train; *right:* Deepest Africa in the River Caves.

white paper cones. Others buy cream-filled waffles. The taste is kids' heaven. The nutritional content is not important, the fun of eating is.

While stuffing our faces we notice that the French Chateau that went under the name Racing Dodgems is constructed of stone, yet the window surrounds are of a tropical fruit motif complete with pineapples. What are tropical fruits doing on a building of sub-arctic architecture? Who cares, we are about to take Dad's car onto the roads where a prang is not punishable with a hiding or jail.

NO BUMPING – ALL CARS IN DIRECTION INDICATED. Huh, what idiot expects that to be observed! The attendant tells us to press the accelerator flat to the floor. Nothing happens...then suddenly, arrh, look out, we all lurch off together. Twenty racing car drivers, Sunday drivers and brown's cows bump their way around the metal-plated track. The blue flash and smell of electricity intensify this myopic mania as does the racket of cast-iron wheels on the steel floor. An attendant clouts a suicidal maniac who has decided to take us all on and head in the opposite direction. When the ride stops we remain in the car, pay the attendant for a second ride and again prove that there is nothing to driving.

Opposite on the Midway and closer to Coney Island, three locomotives charge out of mountains covered with pine trees and snow. Signals move, wheels furiously turn and smoke pours out of the boiler stacks. The central loco rocks in a different direction to the white skeleton that straddles it

Ghost Train, 1935.

with wide red eyes unnervingly matching those of the screaming kids that momentarily bash their way out into the Midway and back again.

A young lad's fear of being called a pansy sucks our group into this nightmare. The desperate screams from within are not from the roller coaster – it must be scary. Clocks above tell the times of our destinations – Hangman's Hill, Creepy Creek, Jittery Juncion, Goofy Gorge, Vampire Vally, Ghastly Gully, Suicide Siding. We are scared stupid even before the attendant puts his hand over a skull and lurches our train ahead, bashing through the first devil-painted doors. Immediately inside we curse our parents for not bearing us with at least one eye in the back of our heads. Crash doors, hard right, crash doors, a skeleton to our side lights up, a scream, around a corner to crash into another car, a violent crashing sound, a series of lights come on showing different parts of bodies, a skeleton jangles. The dark breeds terror. It smells like a musty tomb. We crash though doors to reveal a cage with lions in it, they roar, a man walks past with a torch, I think he is real, we crash though doors, a big dinosaur-like head, a

Watching was as much fun as riding.
– Peter Kingston

Dodgem cars.

horrific roar, more doors, a fire burns, that's not supposed to happen, it's not real, doors, skeletons sit up in front of us, we crash through doors, bats swoop down, we crash through doors, spider webs drape down over us, we crash through doors finally to be out on the Midway for a moment of false respite only to crash back through doors, back into the phosphorescent unknown.

The final heart derailer comes even though we are now certainly out of the tunnel of terror as a volley of 22 shots rings out rattling moving duck-like bits of tin. The Wild West Shooting Gallery is adjacent. My big brother is showing off his marksmanship to a group of young lasses. The ducks aren't the real targets. To think one of them could be his for the price of a plaster kewpie doll.

After having our wits scared out of us, we sure need a laugh. Funnyland sounds like it could be the place.

We feel proud as we pass the long queue to the Dipper. Piece of cake. A machine in Penny Arcade on the right says HERE IT IS – MAGIC CHAIR WITH FOOT EASE. We may need some of that later. I have a quick go on a game that I sit in to operate an aeroplane that gets enough wind blown at it to lift off. Twisting the handles on "The Lightning Strike" shows me on a gauge how much electric current I am withstanding. Youch.

We are drawn into Funnyland by the strange behaviour of people passing behind the two arches over the entrance. Are they walking, tripping, dancing? Whatever it is looks like fun. Above the huge neon-illuminated sign confirms CONEY ISLAND – FUNNYLAND. Which one is it? The latter makes sense as that's what we are after.

We pay our 6d. The sign with clown indicates IF YOU'RE SMALLER THAN ME YOU GET IN FOR FREE. Damn it, when you're young you want to be older and when you're old you want to be younger. Hard left and our leather-soled shoes stampede up the timber steps. The top presents a view back up the Midway to reveal the whole Park with the Bridge and city beyond. I am reminded of the wonderful view from the top of the Big Dipper. What does that mean is next? The strange dancing we saw from outside was another set of jazz boards. The route narrows between handrails on either side over a metal grate. Again air cools us down and forces women's dresses up as strong lights project our images on a wall of canvas for all outside to see.

We are inside this washing machine of fun – people going in every direction. People laughing at themselves and other people laughing at other people laughing. But more of this obstacle course before we get a dose of this. The ramp ends. The only way forward under the slippery slides is over a narrow rope bridge. As always, one uncoordinated dill holds us all up. "Get a move on, drongo." The final stretch presents a floor that drops and vibrates when you step on it, handrails either side of timber rollers on the floor, a floor that moves backward and forward, a floor that is spinning around, a short steep ramp up and down and more gusts of air. Hands clasped with elbows out is the best way through the forest of hoses. We slip through the padded balls with ease but the chubby woman behind thinks the embarrassment is all over when she has poured herself through – only to be exposed with one final blast of air from the floor.

This entry circuit has given us plenty of time to survey the rides and plan a strategy. There is no question – slides first. The first ride is free then we pay. The queue slowly climbs the stair. With the crowd this dense there is no turning back. Holy Toledo! We slide off the precipice with only a coir mat between speed, burns and bums. Guts lift up (no longer slumped down with chips and fairy floss) as our feet lead the charge. Attendants frantically pull people off the red and white striped padded stopper ahead.

Not a moment's rest, we join the Joy Wheel queue. Some of the kids

My best friend screamed so loudly that the bands on her teeth flew out of her mouth.
– Vicki, Castlecrag

The public are funny people.
–Ted Hopkins

I remember being 5 years old and sitting down on the shuffle boards and getting thousands of splinters in my bum.
– Michael, Canberra

I always wore a skirt so that I could do a Marilyn Monroe when walking over the air vents!
– Candace

Midway looking south, 1935.

that can only grab a spot on the edge of the flat cone run for it and rejoin the queue behind us. Once on, the ride operator shouts out "Are you ready?" With increasing speed Coney Island starts to spin around us. One by one the forces of gravity pick off the clinging earthlings as the attendant takes her up through the gears. No one has been king of the castle. One cove thinks he's been gypped as his leg has been grabbed by someone who's lost hold. "By Jesus, I'll thump your bloody..." fists are flying by the time redcoats pick them up by the back of the collar and trousers and throw them out with a warning. This hasn't put a damper on the evening but has shown us to watch our steps.

Staying on the mat was an art to be mastered. One had to preserve modesty and not fall off in the process.
– Nola, Sylvania

The Turkey Trot doesn't interest us so after another descent on the slides we step our way through the revolving Barrels of Fun. In front, feet have been swept out from underneath leaving people helpless to regain

Midway looking south at night, 1935.

The Turkey Trot was hilarious – talk about cheap laughs. Just the funny thing of watching your legs falling away from underneath you seemed hilarious and watching people making fools of themselves.
–Peter Kingston

In the 1930s my sister and I had to be carried out of the two revolving Barrels of Fun. We kept falling down with helpless laughter.

– Shirley, Stanmore

their footing. I put my hands and legs out in a star shape to revolve around upside down. The attendant is quick off the mark, "Eh you, none of that".

After spending quite some time in Coney Island making the most of free admission onto everything other than the slides, the prospect of cool quiet tranquillity leads us to the River Caves. On our right coming out of Coney Island is a huge face with spinning spiral eyes and a lumpy nose that gently moves up and down. It is the Whirler, two-seater cars spinning on an undulating circular track. The attendant rides the track and helps spin the cars even faster, especially for excitable girls.

Next two clowns on enormously long legs stand on either side of a wide striped tent-like facade to the Hey Dey. Girls' hair sweeps out as they spin around the corners, their boyfriends manipulating their grip so as not to crush their girls to death and not miss the opportunity of getting a little bit closer.

Between this and the French Chateau a brass band on a stage ump-pa-pas to a seated audience.

My big brother (with girl in one arm and a photograph of them together sitting on the moon in the other) comes out of the Photographic Studio in the corner of this chocolate box chateau. He obviously has better things to do than speak to us. As he walks off he turns and whispers "River Caves" with the thumbs up gesture, looking sideways at her. We are on the right track.

Goofy House (left), Noah's Ark and Tumble Bug, 1935.

As we wait in the queue, a hook wielded by an attendant pulls up the boats as they come out of the last cavern. The water wheel thrashes as it lifts the water up. The three pairs of couples in the boats wear contented expressions. An endless voice warns "No waiting, no delay, the boats are leaving right away. For your safety folks, keep your hands inside the boat, do not rock the boat and keep the boat level." While getting into the boat we manage to split up some girls so that we each sit next to one of them. This could be a chance to get better acquainted. Up the timber-slatted escalator and then we drop off with a wonderful floating sensation of being free of the ground. It is quiet as the boat gently nudges the sides of the channel as it goes around the corner.

We can hear the arctic winds of the South Pole as we approach a snow-covered hut where a woman in a red outfit waves to a man with a dead reindeer on an old sled dragged by a whole lot of dogs. Another boat goes past on a lower level. There are lots of pointy icicles, a polar bear and penguins.

Through a dark tunnel comes the sound of a howling wolf leading us into the Canadian Rockies. A silhouette of a wolf is projected against an illuminated moon. The sound of bubbling water leads us into an underwater scene with King Neptune and his mermaids in a shell surround. There is so much to look at – apart from whoever you were with and other people in other boats. It is a wonderful thing of total darkness and just feeling the boat nudging and seeing and hearing another land coming. My

A boy would buy a girl an ice cream and take her through the River Caves and squeeze it out of her.

– Ted Hopkins

No matter how hard I tried I never could get that damn boat to tip over!

– Thomas

River Caves, 1935.

mate in front puts his arm around his girl. Her head falls onto his shoulder. Faint heart never won fair maiden so I give it a go. I am promptly told to piss off. What have I done wrong? Perhaps my mate's silly conversations about nothing that did the trick. Never mind.

The sound of "Teddy Bear's Picnic" cheers me up as Toyland approaches. There is a huge rocking horse and Santa Claus making toys with all his helpers. There is a giant rabbit, a barrel that looks like a horse with four sticks as legs on wheels and a ladder up its side with a miniature figure climbing it and things like that. Next real gum trees are a backdrop to Aborigines, koalas and kangaroos. Then into a vast cavern of Deepest Africa with Tarzan and Jane, a lion, emu and a hippopotamus. Tom-toms are beating. Once again past the South Pole and African scenes – seen from a different angle. This time I can make out a couple kissing among the bushes. Not for long as an attendant appears from nowhere in the South Pole. "Eh you. I'll see you outside." A Japanese tea garden drifts by. Shouts, screams and general ruckus preview the final cave – the Park itself.

On the Midway again there is a general movement of people toward the face. The Park is closing. We join in but only to snap up whatever rides we can on the way.

Opposite, south of the French Chateau, a huge pelican perches over the entry to the Whip. A small black figure, a baby or a piccaninny perhaps, stands up in the beak as it opens. Either side of this are laughing faces. The Whip flings out people in circular tubs as they go around the ends of the track. At one end the fear is being flung into the crowds of the Midway; at the other being flung into the harbour. Take your pick. Standing on these revolving ends are two policemen twice life size, with traffic-directing arms extended. The policemen revolve as they direct the traffic that is going around them. We can relate to this sort of nonsense.

That huge insect, the Tumble Bug, is still operating and gives us an opportunity to use up remaining tickets. We all cram in and sit around the edges of an oval-shaped bug looking at each other. As we wait, I notice a beautiful garden in the middle of the ride with real fake stone either side of the rail. Sheer magic as the high seas of Noah's Ark have turned into stone. The bugs move forward then backward several times, then we are off around the undulating track to a whirring sound.

There hasn't been enough time to go on everything. On the train home we brag with others about rides they had taken on. The gentle merry-go-round with its organ and others would have to wait until we have saved up enough money again.

What a night. Ran ourselves ragged, shouted ourselves hoarse, spent all our money – all without our parents – real livin'. As I doze off I wonder where on earth Luna Park had come from. I've heard of Coney Island in America, Luna Park in St Kilda down in Victoria. Adelaide used to have a Luna Park at Glenelg. I wondered if each capital city in Australia (if not the whole world) has a Luna Park. Fantasy has become reality – or was it that reality has become fantasy?

Who cares if the River Caves were tacky, to me they were magic.

–Sharon, Annandale

I particularly recall the River Caves as being the most fantastic journey, of fantastic longing to jump out and meet the Eskimos, the mermaid, the polar bear, King Neptune, Tarzan, etc., in fact I wanted to live there forever."

– Ken, Waverton

1935 Face.

LUNA PARK CONEY ISLAND

THE WORLD'S FIRST

Coney Island is the most human thing that God ever made, or permitted the Devil to make.

–Richard LeGallienne

The origins of Luna Park lie in America. Coney Island New York was undoubtedly the home of the amusement park. Here the biggest, best and most spectacular parks were built. Coney Island was far enough away from Manhattan to be regarded as a holiday resort in the late nineteenth century. On weekends, New Yorkers travelled to the island to enjoy its sun and extensive Atlantic beaches. Following its connection by rail in the 1870s, it had up to 50,000 visitors a day, eager to be entertained.

The first Luna Park built on Coney Island had a legacy which began with the great rivalry that developed between international expositions following the Great Exhibition of 1851 in London. These expositions were conglomerations of the world's people, culture and architecture – all put on show in an effort to show off the countries' produce to encourage trade. The first exposition to have amusements was the 1867 Exposition Universelle in Paris. The Midway, a wide central walkway lined with exhibitions, made its first appearance at the Paris Exposition of 1878 where it was called the *Midway de Plaisance.*

The World's Columbian Exposition in Chicago in 1893–94 had exhibits along a mile-long Midway where exotic buildings competed for attention: a street in Cairo; an Egyptian temple; a Persian palace; a Japanese market and a Turkish village. This assortment of indigenous architectural styles and their method of construction had an enormous influence on amusement parks. Buildings at expositions were built of lath (a thin wood framework on chicken wire base) and staff (a mixture of plaster of Paris and hemp fibre). Plaster of Paris got its name from its extensive use at the 1878 Paris Exposition. The name "White City" arose from the all-white buildings using this kind of construction.

Opposite: Entrance to Luna Park Coney Island.

LUNA PARK
THE HEART OF
CONEY ISLAND
LUNA PARK
THOMPSON & DUNDY
IDLERS
CAFE
RESTAURANT

You see, I have built Luna Park on a definite architectural plan. As it is a place of amusement, I have eliminated all classical conventional forms from its structure, and taken a sort of free Renaissance and Oriental type for my model, using spires and minarets wherever I could, in order to get the festive joyous effect to be derived always from the graceful lines given in this style of architecture. It is marvellous what you can do in the way of arousing human emotions by the use that you can make, architecturally, of simple lines! Luna Park is built on the theory – and the result has proved that theory's truth.

– Frederic Thompson
New York Times, 6 May 1906

I've come to the broad conclusion that what attracts the crowd is the weirdest mind's demand for relief in unconsidered muscular action.

–George C. Tilyou

Exotic cultures and their architectures merged with the carnival when Paul Boyton opened his Sea Lion Park on Coney Island on the Fourth of July 1895. Boyton was already famous as the promoter of an inflatable vulcanised-rubber lifesaving suit. The Park's name came from the 40 sea lions who performed tricks in the central pool. America's first large Shoot-the-Chutes splashed into the same pool. This Park was the first outdoor amusement park to be enclosed by a fence with an admission fee, and also the first where the amusements were run by one person rather than individual showmen running their own concessions.

Another entrepreneur, George Cornelius Tilyou, was so impressed by the first massive Ferris Wheel on the Midway at the Chicago World's Columbian Exposition in 1893 that he ordered an identical wheel half the size. On the strength of his sign ON THIS SITE WILL BE ERECTED THE WORLD'S LARGEST FERRIS WHEEL (the Columbian Exposition wheel having been dismantled), he leased out enough amusement concessions in the surrounding space to enable him to pay for the wheel on delivery. Covered with lights, it was the biggest attraction on Coney Island.

Like Boyton, Tilyou also enclosed his area. But instead of putting up a fence, he constructed a ride that cashed in on Coney Island's most popular sport at the time – horse racing. People raced each other around the Park on timber horses on a metal track. An instant and lasting success, it also gave the Park its name: Steeplechase Park.

The seeds for the world's first Luna Park were sown when Frederic W. Thompson, an architectural draftsman, joined forces with Elmer "Skip" Dundy in Omaha at the 1898 Trans-Mississippi and International Exposition. They met again at the Pan American Exposition in Buffalo, New York in 1901. Together they aggregated $1,500,000 worth of building contracts for amusement structures. The most notable new ride which they built themselves was a cyclorama conceived by Thompson called "A Trip to the Moon".

Thompson's idea probably came from Jules Verne's 1865 *From the Earth to the Moon* as well as H.G. Wells' 1901 *The First Men in the Moon* which was serialised in *Cosmopolitan* magazine. George Melies' 1902 film *A Trip to the Moon* portrays a similar story, borrowing from both Verne and Wells. Melies' film drew large crowds when shown in amusement parks and is accredited as the first science fiction film.

The airship, "Airship Luna", was the archetype that would resonate throughout the rest of Thompson's life and subsequent amusement parks.

> This show was staged in a large building in the centre of which a huge flying machine with large flapping wings was poised on a tower in such a manner that it could be rocked and swayed to imitate a flight in the air... The illusion was aided by projecting scenes and light effects on the inner wall of the building... On finally reaching the moon the gangplank was opened and the patrons perused the lunar landscape which offered many thrills. In one

A Trip to the Moon, 1901.

chamber, with the walls of cheese, a number of active little Brownies scampered about pointing out to the visitors that it was a common belief that the moon was made of cheese, and offered a piece of it to prove the point.
–William F. Mangells, *The Outdoor Amusement Industry from Earliest Times to the Present*

Luna did not actually take off – scenery on three sides was raised and lowered. The illusion was so powerful that some people fainted.

Impressed by their enormous success (400,000 visitors in six months), Tilyou invited Thompson and Dundy to operate "A Trip to the Moon" as a concession at Steeplechase Park in 1902. After a very successful season, they left Tilyou and took over Boyton's unsuccessful Sea Lion Park. Due to the success of the Midway at the World's Columbian Exposition of 1893 and the Pan American Exposition in 1901, they decided to remove all rides except Shoot-the-Chutes and its lagoon and set about creating the first Midway in an amusement park. Thompson conceived and designed the $1,000,000 park that was the pinnacle of amusement parks at the time, and probably forever. On 16 May 1903, 250,000 lights were turned on and Luna Park opened. Forty-three thousand visitors passed through the gates in the first two and a half hours and Thompson and Dundy had paid off all their debts in two months.

All earthly care and trouble can be left a hundred thousand miles behind while the tourist floats onward in the heavens to another world.

– advertisement

You see, this being the moon, it is always changing. A stationary Luna Park would be an anomaly.

– Frederic Thompson

If Paris is France, then Coney Island, between June and September, is the world.
–George C. Tilyou

When opened to the public [Luna Park] caused a sensation in the outdoor amusement field. No park ever received so much acclaim and favourable comment from the press and public, and it created a new era in amusement park development.— William F. Mangells, *The Outdoor Amusement Industry from Earliest Times to the Present*

Such was the impact that Luna Parks have been built all over America and the world, including seven in Australia.

Thompson employed "all the licence in the world". He was obsessed with the ability of the tower to stir the imagination. After four years, Luna Park boasted 1,300,000 electric lights and a total of 1,326 towers, minarets and domes.

The first ride past the entry was "A Trip to the Moon". The Park was centred around a lake into which Shoot-the-Chutes splashed. A few of the many other attractions were: Old Mill, Canals of Venice, A Trip to the North Pole, Dragon's Gorge, Eskimo Village, Monkey Theatre, the Indian Village, Twenty Thousand Leagues under the Sea, War of the Worlds, Chinese Theatre, the Streets of Delhi, Hagenbeck's Animals, and the Mountain Torrent (combination roller coaster and water chute). Spectacular live shows such as Fire and Flames (a four storey building that caught alight every night to be put out by fireman who were really actors) were innovations. Passenger-carrying elephants and camels roamed the Midway along with yaks and 100 horsemen.

A journalist of the time summed it up: "And everywhere was life – a pageant of happy people; and everywhere was colour – wide harmony of orange and white and gold…It was a world removed – shut away from the sordid clatter and turmoil of the streets."

The Park was dramatically altered between seasons. In 1904, 10 million people paid entry to Luna Park.

"A Trip to the Moon" had allowed them this opportunity for success. The name Luna Park was proposed by Elmer Dundy after his sister's christian name, Luna. Thompson agreed because of its reference to his Trip to the Moon.

In 1904, Dreamland opened on Coney Island. Although virtually a copy of Luna Park, it represented a different emphasis, as it was designed for all classes of people, not just the adult proletariat. Attempting to be a permanent exposition, the Park was completely white. Luna Park was of this world and beyond. Dreamland was a world under the sea entered beneath a giant plaster of Paris ship in full sail. The Park was adorned with 1,000,000 lights.

Between Luna Park and Dreamland, one could experience almost any part of the universe – certainly a novelty before television, film and world travel became accessible.

In 1907, Steeplechase Park burnt to the ground. Immediately Tilyou began building a new park on the site. Tilyou had the ability to know what entertainment people wanted, when they wanted it and what would make

them come back again and again. To further test his theory that people would pay almost any price to amuse themselves and to be laughed at by others in the same predicament, he put various rides inside a huge steel and glass building called the Pavilion of Fun. This was an innovation as the appeal of both Luna Park and Dreamland was that they were themselves spectacular shows. Tilyou allowed people to have fun by being the show.

Luna Park Coney Island.

Tilyou also realised that in an amusement environment, emotions could be more openly expressed. The amusements inside the Pavilion of Fun explored these ideas. One entrance was through the "Barrel of Love". This revolving barrel meant that unfamiliar people were forcibly brought together by their inability to balance. Another entry had a clown and a

Luna Park Heliopolis, Egypt.

dwarf greeting visitors on a brightly lit stage where men were startled by mild electric shocks while women were embarrassed by having their skirts blown up by air shooting out of the floor while an audience looked on.

Outside the Pavilion of Fun, most rides were rebuilt, including the steeplechase ride (although with only with four tracks and metal horses). Tilyou introduced the combination ticket which admitted the holder to practically all the attractions in the Park at less than the total cost of buying tickets for each one separately. His theories proved to be law – the Park was now doing better than ever.

In 1907, Dundy, Luna Park's manager and accountant, died. Thompson spent money extravagantly on yachts and unsuccessful Broadway productions but little on Luna Park.

A fire in 1911 which started at the dark indoor ride called "Hell Gate" took only three hours to totally destroy Dreamland, which was never rebuilt.

In 1912, Thompson, now a heavy drinker, lost Luna Park to his creditors and died bankrupt in 1919. Although renovated in 1935 and 1941, Luna Park, with businessmen at the helm, failed to succeed. No new rides were added and old rides were poorly maintained. A fire in 1946 destroyed half the Park, another in 1947 destroyed "A Trip to the Moon" and finally in 1949 the Luna Park site was cleared for a housing development.

The Steeplechase and its Pavilion of Fun were removed in 1966. Only the structure of the Parachute tower remains.

At their beginnings and during their heydays, amusement parks were virtually the only type of mass popular entertainment available. As menageries became permanent zoos, travelling repertory companies found permanent theatres and travelling bioscopes were replaced by cinemas, amusement park patrons began to fall in numbers.

When mass transport spread, people could go on holiday to places that were previously only imitated in parks and fairs. After World War I, telephones, gramophones, radio and cars were more readily available. As a result people wanted faster and more thrilling rides with more flashing lights, colour and chrome.

Of the 1,500 amusement parks that existed in America in 1919, only 500 were operating in 1930. The Great Depression shut many parks. A slight revival occurred in the 1940s due to World War II, but the final decline started in the early 1950s with the spread of television.

Amusement parks were always doomed. They were never built as permanent fixtures. As novelty wore off and trends changed, so did the rides. Because of this intrinsic impermanence, cheap materials and methods were used. Constant vandalism shut many parks as maintenance, replacement and security became too costly. But fire was the greatest single contributor to their downfall.

Amusement parks rose to popularity due to their ability to change and present the latest technological inventions in the form of rides. Their downfall was due to the proliferation of technology which created alternatives for mass entertainment.

LUNA PARK ST KILDA

AUSTRALIA'S FIRST

The first mention of an Australian Luna Park was in a 1906 *Billboard* magazine which referred to Frederick Ingersoll having "architects and designers at work on plans for parks in England and Australia for a French syndicate". Nothing seems to have come of these plans. In 1912 (nine years after Luna Park Coney Island opened), American entrepreneurs involved in the early Australian film industry proposed the idea of a Luna Park at St Kilda.

Luna Park St Kilda is the link between Australia and America. Australia must have appeared as a new frontier to the Americans who were active in the film industry in Australia when the potential of film and recreation in general was beginning to become evident. Technological innovation was increasingly being applied to entertainment and leisure.

Luna Park St Kilda was the Australian testing ground where ideas were imported, created and made real, refined or scrapped. The knowledge gained there was passed on to Luna Parks at Glenelg and Milsons Point and, to some degree, to other parks such as White City.

Like Coney Island, St Kilda was a popular seaside resort, particularly following its connection to Melbourne by railway in 1854 and tram in 1891. For some time the only carnival-type attraction was Baxter's merry-go-round, until the musical comedy *The English Pierrots* was presented in 1904. Their success attracted a carousel, a roller skating rink, donkey rides and a miniature railway in 1905. In 1906, J. and N. Tate made the world's first feature length movie *The Story of the Kelly Gang* on the land that was to become Luna Park.

On 2 November 1906, St Kilda's first amusement park, Dreamland, was opened on just over two hectares on the Luna Park site. The Park was

MAIN ENTRANCE
WHITE CITY SYDNEY

adorned with white-painted pagodas and minarets surrounded with a 2.4 metre high fence. Of particular interest among the various attractions was a copy of Frederic Thompson's "A Trip to the Moon in an Air-Ship".

Public apathy and poor attractions (the *Truth* newspaper dubbed it "Deadland") forced Dreamland to close after only one summer season. The site remained disused with the structures still standing.

Since 1904, the Canadian James Dixon Williams had been showing movies in a blacktop tent in Vancouver and several other North American cities. Arriving penniless in Sydney in 1909, he survived by selling novelty walking sticks. He borrowed money to lease the Oxford Theatre, renovated and reopened it as the Colonial in 1910. Unlike his competitors, he built luxurious cinemas around Australia, introducing continuous shows and imported films. His Lyric Theatre was the first big motion picture theatre in the world, seating 2,000.

In May 1911 the Greater J.D. Williams Amusement Company Limited leased the Dreamland site and made a proposal to erect a Steeplechase Park like the one at Coney Island with a ride of artificial horses surrounding the Park. A scenic railway was added to the proposal in July. The Steeplechase ride was withdrawn in January 1912 as it was considered unsafe for women and children. Instead the Old Mill, House of Illusions and Sliding Bowl were added.

In the same month Luna Park Limited was formed as a subsidiary of the Greater J.D. Williams Amusement Company with J.D. Williams as managing director and Herman Phillips as manager. Herman Phillips was the eldest and most entrepreneurial of three brothers. Leon came to Australia with Herman from America, and Harold, the youngest, followed a year later.

Later in 1912 Williams and Phillips opened the Palais Pictures across the road from Luna Park after demolishing a "Figure 8" roller coaster that had opened five years earlier.

T.H. Eslick as engineer-in-chief was responsible for the design and construction of Luna Park St Kilda. He had spent 14 years building amusement parks all over the world (for L.A. Thompson in Broadway, New York; for G.A. Lawsha of London; for Scenic Railways in London, Yarmouth, New Brighton, Blackpool, Edinburgh and Vienna; as well as the Brussels Exhibition and the Royal Indian Durbar Exhibition in Bombay and Luna Parks in Vienna, Paris, Cairo, Cologne, Berlin and St Petersburg).

Twenty American fun fair experts were among the workmen. The building contractors were Messrs G.A. Lawsha of London. V. Churchill was the scenic artist. Whitney Bros. were the main concessionaires at both Luna Park Coney Island and Luna Park St Kilda.

On the superstitious day of Friday, 13 December 1912, 15,000 lights were turned on as Luna Park St Kilda was opened by the Minister for Foreign Affairs, Josiah Thomas. The Lord Mayor of Melbourne and Mayor of St Kilda were also among the dignitaries. The evening concluded with Herr Granado and Mme Fedora (who had worked with Ringling Bros. and Barnum & Bailey's circuses) performing "The Human Wire-Walking Elephant".

Above: Scenic Railway; *left:* The Palace of Illusions; *opposite top:* Entrance to Luna Park St Kilda, c. 1912; *opposite bottom:* Entrance to White City, Rushcutters Bay.

Luna Park holds all the thrills modern science can produce, has the biggest Scenic Railway Ride ever built, contains the only Bowl slide built outside America, was designed and built by one of the most capable contractors in the business, holds the largest and most elaborate Tea Terrace Garden in Australia and will be crowded nightly and be an assured success from the moment her spacious gates are flung open – because that is the Williams' way.

– opening advertisement

Above: Human Wire-Walking Elephant above Luna Park St Kilda, 1912;
below: Postcard from the Electric Studio.

Attendance on opening night was 22,319 people and on both the Friday and Saturday nights people had to be turned away from the gates.

Gold chariots just outside the entry changed money as they had at Luna Park Coney Island. The entrance to the Park was through an enormous 10 metre diameter cement render and chicken wire face known as Mr Moon or Mr Luna. At the opening, the eyes were illuminated and rolled from side to side to

> *...express Mr Moon's joy in being at last able to get down amongst those humans in whose love affairs he is supposed to have taken a fatherly interest since the first song writer wrote the first love song – and ran short of a snappy rhyme for "coon".* – souvenir

The Pan American Exposition in Buffalo had an exhibit called Dreamland where one entered under a giant face. Luna Park on Coney Island had a funhouse called the Pit, also entered under a huge laughing man's face with narrow tall towers on either side. Funhouses at Luna Park in Cleveland, Ohio and Steeplechase Park in Atlantic City were also entered through a face.

On either side of the face were towers with Arabic embellishments. The Scenic Railway, designed by L.A. Thompson Scenic Railway Company of New York, passed through the tops of these towers and over the top of the face, then dipped and curved around the Park's triangular boundary. The slogan of L.A. Thompson's revolutionary "Oriental Scenic Railway" at Atlantic City – RIDE IT JUST FOR FUN – was the source of

Giggle Palace.

Luna Park St Kilda and later Milsons Point's slogan JUST FOR FUN. Queues to the Scenic Railway (and later the Big Dipper) were often three deep and 100 metres long.

Behind the entrance towers and Palais de Folies was the American Bowl Slide, only the third of its kind in the world. Patrons were carried to the top of the slide on moving chairs, then sat on mats and slid down into a giant spectator-surrounded bowl "from which it will require ingenuity to escape". A large Canadian lumber mill sent boats into the River Caves of the World on a voyage of discovery through underground grottoes.

Luna Park St Kilda's manager, Louis A. Corbeille, designed and built Pharoah's Daughter and other illusions in the Park based on those he had invented for Dreamland on Coney Island. Pharoah's Daughter was an Egyptian building entered between two stone sphinxes. Inside was a large auditorium with seats and a proscenium; illusions were presented on the stage. The Palace of Illusions, next to Pharoah's Daughter, contained eight more illusions.

The glories of the Taj Mahal, the grandeur of the Alps, the quaintness of old Japan, the gaiety of the Mont-Martre [sic], the beauties of the ocean bed and the amusement side of the Wembly [Wembley] Exhibition, are to be seen at Luna Park, St Kilda. Tonight admission is free to these wonderful sights. Among the novelties secured from Wembley is a ball game which is named "Bulls-eyed out of Bed". By an ingenious device, an alluring lady, clad in the daintiest of night attire, is tumbled out of bed.

– 1924 ad

Above: Luna Park St Kilda, Palais Pictures and Palais de Danse; *right:* Midway with River Caves and Dodgem Building (left).

For him [J.D. Williams] Australia was a place of delightful climate peopled by working classes who had more money to spend on amusement than the average American and more time to spend it in. His object was to establish a popular resort where people of all classes could find regular and frequent enjoyment at prices that would not make their pleasure a drain on their resources.

– Lone Hand, 1 July 1911

Australians are entitled to the best amusements in the world because they are the best amusement public in the world.

– J.D. Williams
at the opening of Luna Park St Kilda

Shows during the opening season included the Curious Flea Circus, Electro and Electra who gave electrical demonstrations, Baby Ben as the World's Fattest Boy, weighing 351 pounds at age 12, and Siamese twins, Daisy and Violet Hilton.

Other acts included Ardo the Human Frog (a contortionist who vied with mermaids in the River Caves), the Osleon Brothers (Human Spinning Tops) and Louina and Franzy who performed feats on the high wire as well as their Slide For Life – hanging by their teeth down a wire suspended from the entrance towers. A Swedish diver from Luna Park Coney Island, Miss Marie Thelin, nightly took a 15 metre plunge with her clothes alight into a 3 metre tank of blazing water. On 24 January 1913, Harley Davidson who held countless records and titles throughout the world for roller and ice skating (as well as motor cycling) gave a roller skating display to 7,000 spectators.

Inside the Palais des Folies (later the Giggle Palace) was a revolving barrel, a Devil's Staircase, Distorting Mirrors, Slippery Dips, various trip wire gadgets and the "Electric Studio" where patrons could be photographed by Messrs Whitney Bros in a number of different scenes such as sitting in a car in front of the Luna Park gates. The Whitney Bros were the originators of the first practical "while-you-wait" photographic system in the world. They are also credited with the first use of cartoon cutouts through which people stuck their heads for character photos. Coney Island Crispettes could be eaten inside the Palais des Folies and reproductions of Caruso's and Melba's voices could be heard inside in the Dome of Music.

Change had to be given for the 150 American slot machines which only operated with American coins. The American Soda Fountain was popular, and special American dishes were served on the Tea Terrace above the River Caves. Catering for 2,000 patrons, the Terrace offered a view of Luna Park to one side and "the moon-bleached waters of the harbour" of Port Phillip Bay to the other.

The Luna Park Band, conducted by R.H. McAnally, played everything from waltzes to marches, including the Luna Park theme song:

A balmy night, a merry lark,
A pretty girl and Luna Park.

The first season operated until 26 April 1913. During this time 439,000 people paid sixpence admission. During the winter the Park was overhauled and maintained.

In 1913 the three major Australian film exhibitors, Cozens Spencer, T.J. West and J.D. Williams, amalgamated to form Union Theatres which later became Greater Union. In the winter of 1913 Williams returned to America after releasing Luna Park St Kilda to the control of Lieut.-Colonel John Monash (chairman of directors), Herman F. Phillips (amusement manager), Gerald Robinson and Percy Cook (directors) and A.C. Sutherland (secretary). In 1917 Williams started the First National Pictures Corporation which was later acquired by Warner Bros. Williams later signed Hollywood's first million dollar contract – with Charlie Chaplin.

I am satisfied that I have given clean pleasure, real home enjoyment under proper control to many many thousands of young people.

– Herman Phillips 1916

You'd have thought he [Herman] was a Hollywood director. He used to go around with a big cigar in his mouth and a big hat and everybody would jump to attention when he would come in. He had everything very much in hand. He was the big boss. He was bigger than life.

– Merle, North Caulfield

Top: Water Chute; *above:* Jack and Jill.

After Luna Park, Eslick built and managed White City in Rushcutters Bay, Sydney, which opened on 3 December 1913 with attractions similar to those at Luna Park. White City was owned by Cozens Spencer and was on the same site as his film studio. Of particular note was their Philadephia Toboggan Company carousel No. 30, the only PTC carousel to leave America. The order form for this carousel is addressed to "Luna Park (Mr Spencer), Sydney, Australia". In *Tabletalk* magazine in December 1912, J.D. Williams announced that Sydney was to have its own Luna Park. White City may at one time have been proposed to have been called Luna Park, and Spencer's one-time rivalry, then association, with J.D. Williams may have prevented his use of the name.

Few major changes were made for the 1913–14 season. Some River Caves scenes were changed and added such as the scene of Burke and Wills' expedition modelled from a painting at the National Gallery. The success of Luna Park's 1913-14 season depended upon the novelty of the new attractions and the advertising campaign prior to the end of the season:

L*imitless Laughter,*
U*ndiluted Delight*
N*ewest Novelties*
A*rtistic Attractions*

P*erpetual Pleasure*
A*ll for Fun*
R*ejuvenating Joy Jaunts*
K*eep you Smiling.*

During the winter of 1914 moving pictures were shown in the Palais des Folies, now called the Lounge. The most popular show that season was Kaiser's Kitchen, where people hurled crockery at an effigy of the Kaiser. As a substitute for expensive overseas acts (made difficult to get by the war) many carnivals were presented including a Fancy Dress Carnival, a Battle of Confetti, an Auld Lang Syne Carnival and a Carnival of the Allies.

Due to the war, Luna Park was closed for the 1915–16 season except for the Scenic Railway and Palais des Folies (now called Merryland) which were kept open all year. Many a last night before going off to war was spent at Luna Park.

Except for charity concerts, the Park was closed for the rest of the war, as new rides and replacement parts were unobtainable due to shipping and manufacturing restrictions. This was followed by a dispute over the lease which kept the Park closed until October 1923.

During 1922 Leon Phillips visited America and England. Work began in August 1923 on the installation of the Big Dipper (designed by Miller & Baker Inc., Connecticut: John A Miller was known as the master roller coaster designer for the Philadelphia Toboggan Company), the Whip (designed by W.F. Mangels of Coney Island) and the Water Chute. A £15,000 Philadelphia Toboggan Company carousel (consisting of 68 horses four abreast and two chariots decorated with a war and peace theme) that had been in Sydney's White City was acquired and adorned with 6,000 lights.

About this time Rupert Browne joined the adjoining Palais Pictures as scenic artist. Browne had studied at Drury Lane Art School in London after the war while waiting to be returned to Australia. In the Palais he worked

Top: Philadelphia Toboggan Company carousel; *above:* Splash-O and Noah's Ark.

...half forgotten secrets, the intangible charm, the world of magic and mystery that once entertained and awed the Egyptian courts of ages long since gone.

– souvenir

There was a young man from Footscray
To DODGEM *he ran all the way*
He'd heard it was great
So through Luna Park gate
*He dashed, shouting wildly, "*HOORAY*".*

Opposite: The Rotor.

on a massive scale on distorted perspectives that would assist him when designing the fantasy for Luna Park.

The opening of the "New Luna Park" in October 1923 was preceded by a massive advertising campaign of a kind never before seen in Melbourne. The opening poster read:

> *Your life must not be lived in vain*
> *See Luna Park – you'll smile again.*

For the first time advertising was aimed at children who were admitted free to Saturday matinees. Only the Scenic Railway and the River Caves remained essentially the same as before the war.

In 1925 and 1934 the Park was opened during the winter for the visiting American fleet. Dodgems were introduced in 1926 following negotiations commenced by Leon Phillips during his visit to America in 1922. They consisted of eighteen two-man cars and were located above the Whip in the Dodgem Pavilion with its distinctive French chateau architecture.

In 1928 a Jack and Jill and Goofy House were added. New attractions for the 1934–35 season were the Bug, the Caterpillar and the Pretzel which in 1937 was transformed into the Ghost Train. As a response to the Big Band Era, many band competitions were sponsored during the 1935–36 and 1936–37 seasons.

For the 1937–38 season, the carousel became a huge birthday cake, adorned with 25 huge coloured candles to celebrate 25 years of the Park's operation. It was also a requiem for Herman Phillips.

During World War II only minor rides were added. The Park was especially popular with American soldiers and their girlfriends. The Park's lights had special fittings to camouflage the lights in case of enemy attack. Again the amusement manufacturing industry was stagnant during and immediately after the war.

It was not until 1951 that major changes were made. An electricity generating plant was installed to overcome frequent power restrictions. The Rotor was installed following its success in Sydney. Jack and Jill, the Carousel Building, the Dodgems and the Whirler were reconstructed.

In 1953 the Park, especially the face, was refurbished for the coronation of Queen Elizabeth.

When the two remaining Phillips brothers, Leon and Harold, died in 1957, their shares were sold by their American relatives and the Park declined steadily thereafter. In 1987 the Hyams family (relatives of Luna Park's financial backers the Abrahams) sold their shares, ending an era.

Following the 1979 fire at Sydney's Luna Park, the River Caves were considered unable to be made fireproof. They were demolished and replaced by the Hurricane from Sydney in late 1980. On 27 November 1981, a fire destroyed the Shoot 'em Gallery as well as the company's offices and part of the Giggle Palace.

Luna Park St Kilda is acclaimed as the world's oldest amusement park under one management. Its Scenic Railway boasts being the world's oldest operating roller coaster.

ROTOR
RIDE THE ROTOR
ROTOR

1930 Luna Park Glenelg in background:
Big Dipper Station (left), Noah's Ark, Goofy
House, River Caves (right), with Big Dipper
behind.

LUNA PARK GLENELG
SOUTH AUSTRALIA'S FIRST

Like Coney Island, St Kilda and Manly, Glenelg was a seaside resort in Adelaide far enough from the city by tram to provide relief from everyday life.

David Atkins, the Phillips brothers, Ted Hopkins and Rupert Browne, the vital personalities who were to create Sydney's Luna Park, first came together at Glenelg:.

David Atkins started in the amusement business working for his elder brother, Jack, who was one of the biggest outdoor showmen in South Australia. At the age of 23 in 1925, David Atkins took over an open air picture theatre in Port Pirie and set up five stalls, a merry-go-round, horse-o-plane and Ferris wheel as concessions. After two successful years he sold out and took a travelling show to Broken Hill before heading for Sydney where he established the Big Wheel Grounds (featuring a 24 metre high Ferris wheel) at Manly with Charles Nelson and Harry Stiller.

Several successful years ended when their site was sold. Subsequently Harold Spry started Luna Park Manly on the site. David Atkins, who for a time had the amusement rights for Coogee and Manly piers, would obtain the rights to the name Luna Park from Harold Spry in 1935.

In March 1928, Mr T.S. Gordon applied to erect a Luna Park north of Wrigley Reserve in Glenelg with a scenic railway, water chute, maze, Katzanjammer Castle, Witching Waves and Rubber-de-dub (which was to be imported from Luna Park Paris). Gordon claimed to have had experience in similar amusements at Marseilles and White City in London. Although the scheme did not proceed, in July 1929 the Council resolved to advertise an area on Colley Reserve for the operation of a scenic railway.

David Atkins was awarded the lease in October 1929 and in February

We were really amazed at the public response. It was the first time Sydney people had seen our type of amusement park, and they liked it. We had Australia's largest Ferris wheel, and soon introduced dodgem cars, which were then an absolute novelty. The success we had there set me thinking about the possibilities of a gigantic amusement park in Sydney. I suppose you could say the idea of Luna Park was born there.
– David Atkins

Above: The rear of Luna Park Glenelg; *right:* Games in Penny Arcade.

I liked to place my hand on the machine and have my fortune told.

– Joyce, Ashford

Offices (left), Penny Arcade, Big Dipper Station, Noah's Ark and River Caves.

1930 was allowed to add the Goofy House, Noah's Ark and several slot machines. Prior to this, David Atkins had met Australia's amusement park giant of the day, Herman Phillips, and the two men clicked. He was able to convince Herman Phillips to consider an amusement park at Glenelg Beach. Luna Park Glenelg Ltd was formed and the Phillips and Abraham brothers built Luna Park Glenelg with David Atkins as manager.

Ted Hopkins was an electrical engineer who had worked for seven years at a tin mine in Renison Tasmania where he learned to "make do with what was available". When tin prices fell and the mine closed, he travelled to Melbourne to look for work. He met Trevor Hedberg, the consulting engineer for Luna Parks St Kilda and Glenelg, who offered him a job at Glenelg. Hopkins responded "You give me a fare there and back and I'll go across there". He joined Luna Park Glenelg as maintenance engineer a week before the Park opened, and worked on the electrical installation.

The Park (like St Kilda before and Milsons Point in the future) was built on reclaimed land. A sea wall was built on beach-edge dunes with the reclamation done by the council and paid for by Luna Park Glenelg Ltd.

Hundreds of unemployed used to stand around each day and watch the progress. If there was a hint of any men being put on, the line-up would be hundreds. There was no dole in those days, nothing for us single men and only ration tickets for the married.
– Frank, Glenelg

A woman got drunk at one of the pubs and she said she was going to jump out of the Big Dipper and she did.

– Ted Hopkins

[She fell 10 metres onto the second big curve. David Atkins and Ted Hopkins pulled her off the tracks before the train could run her over.]

Above right: Big Dipper Station; *below:* Props from the Palais Pictures St Kilda set, designed by Rupert Browne, were used in Toyland.
Opposite top: Deepest Africa in the River Caves; *below:* Toyland in the River Caves.

Luna Park Glenelg was designed by Rupert Browne in the form of an esplanade with no surrounding fence or point of entry. Not to be upstaged by the ocean outlook, the attractions turned their backs on the beach and view. During construction £37,600 was spent, 130 men toiled and 40 kilometres of electrical cable, 10,000 light bulbs and 75,000 lineal metres of timber were used. The River Caves alone consumed 50 tonnes of plaster of Paris.

On 8 October 1930, Glenelg's Mayor J.W. Sutherland introduced the Attorney-General of South Australia, W.J. Denny, who officially opened Luna Park Glenelg.

Rides at the opening included the Big Dipper, the Goofy House, the River Caves (also known as the Old Mill), Noah's Ark and the Penny Arcade. Rides were 6d except the Big Dipper which was 9d.

Much of the mechanics were made in Luna Park St Kilda. The Big Dipper and station were identical to St Kilda's. The Goofy House had a Haunted Swing as well as a flea circus with fleas harnessed by thin wire to a small cart. As they jumped, they pulled the cart. Only human fleas could be used and consequently the fleas had to feed on their owner's arms and legs. The River Caves scenes were designed and modelled by Messrs J. & W. Rowell, artists who had also worked at Luna Park St Kilda. The contents of Toyland in the River Caves was from a set at the Palais Theatre by Rupert Browne.

For four years the Park ran smoothly, making satisfactory profits during the hardship of the Great Depression. However, the Park never enjoyed cooperation from the council or local residents, who claimed the Park was

a haven for carnival types and undesirables. Council would not allow changes or expansion. The issue came to a head when an application to open the River Caves on Sunday was rejected. David Atkins claimed that this was necessary to keep the whole venture from failing.

Anticipating further trouble, David Atkins explored alternative sites and when he found a site in Sydney, Luna Park Glenelg Ltd was placed in voluntary liquidation in late 1934 and put up for auction on 8 April 1935. The directors claimed that even if they had the site rent-free, they could not make it pay. The council released the company from the remaining years of its lease.

Conveniently, the directors of the company bought all the equipment. Ted Hopkins made drawings of the rides and 1,300 tonnes of rides were numbered, dismantled and packed on board the specially chartered *Mungana* which left Port Adelaide for Sydney on 14 June 1935.

LUNA PARK MILSONS POINT

SYDNEY'S OWN

Ted Hopkins claimed that Luna Park Milsons Point at its opening was 15 years ahead of its time and was the best lit park he had ever seen. Separated from the city by the waters of the harbour and the massive arching Harbour Bridge, Luna Park had a unique position. No other amusement park in the world could boast such a location.

The cliff face as a blank curtain and the black of the night was the perfect background on which a fantastic world could be painted with shape, colour and light. At night, the lights on the water doubled the effect.

But the site had many uses before Luna Park. A rocky shoreline with residences of watermen who operated the ferry service between Dawes Point and Milsons Point was first quarried to make way for the North Shore rail line extension to Milsons Point in 1893. In 1915, pending construction of the Harbour Bridge, the Milsons Point railway station was moved there from the road/ferry/rail interchange on Milsons Point. When contracts were signed in 1924 for the construction of a bridge across Sydney Harbour, the station was moved northwest on the Lavender Bay foreshore to make room for the construction factory of bridge contractors Dorman Long and Company. To accommodate this factory, the cliff was further quarried to its present alignment, the shore line was filled and straightened and a wharf (on which the present Dodgem Building stands) and workshops were built. J.J.C. Bradfield, designer of the Harbour Bridge, proposed a long building with extensive hanging gardens for the Lavender Bay foreshore.

The Harbour Bridge was opened on 19 March 1932. In December 1933, Mr A.M. Pickford, a New Zealand businessman, proposed an amusement park on the Dorman Long site with a Scenic Railway that would encircle the park, Whip, River Caves, Dodgems, Water Dodgems, Joy Wheel,

Midway looking north, 1935.

I like that easy confrontation of elite and mass cultures, the fun fair and the temple, whose symbol in Sydney is Luna Park facing the Opera House across the harbour.

– *Robert Hughes*, Time

Top: Milsons Point Station, c. 1894;
above: Dorman Long factory

Caterpillar and carousel. He had an option to purchase these rides from Luna Park Auckland. The government responded that "an amusement park of the type suggested is not in keeping with the dignity with which the approaches to [as] important a structure as the Sydney Harbour Bridge should be associated".

When David Atkins (from Luna Park Glenelg) was having problems with the Glenelg Council in 1933, he went to Sydney to search (unsuccessfully) for a suitable site on a beach or near the city. The next year he returned to Sydney: "My wife and I walked our feet sore looking for land, but we could find nothing worthwhile. Councils in the beach areas didn't appreciate the value of the park we planned and gave us no cooperation. After several months we were ready to give up, but decided to see one more block before we left for Melbourne. It was the old site of Dorman and Long's Harbour Bridge workshop adjacent to the northern pylon. I had noticed it many times but thought it was too small. Well, we went down among the weeds and measured it, and found to our surprise that it was 5.5 acres."

In April 1934, the government response to a proposal from Harry Musgrove to erect an amusement park on the site was that it had not determined the use of this land. A flood of proposals followed from Luna Park Glenelg, A.M. Pickford, J.C. Brendrodt and R.W. Marsh.

The government considered and North Sydney Council agreed that the land under the Bridge, in addition to their existing park land, was all that

Left: Bradfield's proposal for Lavender Bay, 1924; *below:* Dorman Long factory being dismantled and pontoon that was to become the Palais de Danse, 1932.

could be economically maintained. An amusement park, along with a proposed municipal pool, would stimulate commercial activity in the area. This in turn would attract traffic over the Bridge which was failing to pay its way.

When tenders for use of the Lavender Bay site were called by the Department of Main Roads, the Mayor of Willoughby claimed "the amusement park would deteriorate property and attract an undesirable element into the area". A petition with 1,000 signatures from the people of North Sydney was presented to the government opposing commercial use of the land. Reverend Calder said that "if a Luna Park of any description were erected here it might become a menace to the morals and well-being of the people of the district. There would be nightly orgies there which could not be checked". Protesters claimed that "the proposal was like putting Coney Island under the Tower of London", that Coney Island was one of the world's worst "sinks" and that "It will be another unnecessary ugly blot on our foreshores".

Prior to the tender submission date, Herman Phillips paid several visits to other tenderers and the Department of Main Roads, objecting to the proposed lease conditions as well as stating that he would not be submitting a tender as, from his extensive experience, the rent was too great to support the development. While attempting to scare off opposition, he made his objections to the lease clear, made the Department aware of his credentials and suggested how other tenders should be scrutinised. He also offered his assistance to the Department.

Tenders were received in July 1934 from: William Scott and A.A. Abrahams (Phillips' financial partner); J.C. Brendrodt; Archer Whitford; Harry Musgrove; and Luna Park Ltd (Herman Phillips). Phillips' was the only tender to propose Olympic Drive as the entry point. The highest tender from Harry Musgrove was accepted. When it was revealed that Musgrove was an undisclosed bankrupt, Herman Phillips disclosed that he was also a member of that syndicate and the project was re-tendered with an amended lease.

Herman Phillips didn't know what he wanted till he got it. But when he got it, he knew. Herman Phillips was right.
– Ted Hopkins

No other park in the world has an entrance compared with what ours was like.

– Ted Hopkins

Above: Stuart Bros construction drawings, 1935; *opposite:* 1935 face.

I probably put in more lamps than anybody else in bloody Australia. If I didn't put it in, Eddie Devine would have.

–Dick Pearce

Do you know that Luna Park's 40,000 light bulbs use as much electricity as the town of Gundagai?

– David Atkins

It [chicken wire] hides a multitude if sins.

– Ted Hopkins

Only one tender was received in March 1935 – from Herman Phillips. The tender did not include any plans or description of rides, only the term and rent. The lease for 20 years was signed by Herman Phillips and Emmanuel Abrahams who formed Luna Park (NSW) Ltd. Leases were then negotiated with the Department of Railways for extra land on which Coney Island was to be built and for the use of the wharf from the Sydney Harbour Trust.

Alderman Stanton from North Sydney Council supported the proposal – "the city needs brightening and more amusements: Luna Park would supply a big want in the lives of the people of Sydney and North Sydney". In the same year a proposal to build a Luna Park at Bondi had been rejected by the local Council.

The equipment from Luna Park Glenelg was off-loaded in late June by a temporary crane on the Dorman Long wharf and stored in a building that would later be the Ghost Train. Work started in July 1935.

The layout of Luna Park is accredited to Herman Phillips whose vague ideas were realised and given their artistic imagination by Rupert Browne, designer of Luna Park Glenelg and scenic artist for the Palais Pictures in St Kilda.

David Atkins, who had been instigator and manager of Luna Park Glenelg, was the manager responsible for the Park's construction. Stuart Bros were the building contractors.

Ted Hopkins, the maintenance engineer and assistant manager, made Browne's conceptions work, both mechanically and electrically. Rupert Browne returned to Melbourne following the opening of the Park, leaving Arthur Barton to continue the scenic painting in the Park.

This "City of a Million Lights" was built at a cost of £60,000 by 800 structural employees and 35 artists plus labourers and fitters using 750,000 metres of timber and 60,000 bags of cement. The whole central walkway of three hectares was paved in four days. Buildings were constructed with such haste that Council approval was generally gained during construction or on completion. Hundreds of out-of-work skilled tradesmen, many of whom had previously worked on the Harbour Bridge, would line up outside the gates for Stuart Bros to take their pick.

With a team of 70 electricians, Ted Hopkins carried out the electrical installation in only six weeks. At that time he was nicknamed the "White Cloud" because of the speed with which he rushed up and down the length of the Park "watching this and watching that". He installed one side of the Park while the electrical foreman from Luna Park St Kilda installed the other. They outlined the Park's features with thousands of small light bulbs (each etched with "Luna Park") of 11 volts and 5 watts at roughly 250 mm intervals. Three hundred metres of neon tube were used in the Park.

Unlike most amusement parks, people came from the suburbs into Sydney to be amused. Its central location meant that there was abundant transport. For the opening, a free ferry service of the *Kuttabul* and *Koompartoo* ferries sponsored by Luna Park operated from Circular Quay to Luna Park.

LUNA PAR
CLOSED
DURING WINTER MONTHS
RE-OPEN SEPTEMBER 30TH

Below: David Atkins; *right:* Big Boy.

When they were building that I used to be up there with the electricians and that and the neon people. There was a chap working for the neon people, he was only about 19 and he used to sing all day and they'd say "Shut up! Shut up!" and he'd be singin' away there all day and I used to love hearing him sing. Tex Morton. Country and western. He's famous. He used to have a horse there in Martin Place and put the hat down and do a bit of buskin'.

– Jack, Cabramatta

They were pouring the concrete paving a week before the park opened. They were working night and day. There were blokes pushing these big barrows along all mixed on site by Stuart Bros.

– Jack, Cabramatta

Milsons Point Station was now located in Alfred Street, a short walk to the giant gate adorned with incandescent bulbs and a neon sign proclaiming: ENTRANCE LUNA PARK AND OLYMPIC POOL. The gate previewed the Park. It was probably the only privately-owned piece of advertising spanning a public street in Sydney. It was allowed by North Sydney Council as a gesture of gratitude to Luna Park which gave employment to more than 1,000 men during the Depression. For many years after the opening of Luna Park, Council also allowed free parking for 1,000 cars on the lawn of Bradfield Park south of this gate. A man in a white coat parked the cars.

The only public access to Luna Park was past the North Sydney Olympic Pool through the face. The remaining boundaries (the railway yards, the harbour and the cliff face) provided excellent cover for the backs of what was unashamedly facade architecture. The Park was insulated from the real world (and visa versa) except through the face.

The face and towers, designed by Rupert Browne, were based on Luna Park St Kilda's moon face. The face characterisation (especially Arthur Barton's later renovation) and radiating tiara-like aurora from its forehead were reminiscent of George Tilyou's smiling face at Steeplechase Park on Coney Island. These smiling faces were their Park's trademarks. At Luna Park, your trust was left with the face. The serious, real, conforming, regulated outside world was washed off to enter into the body of frivolity, fantasy and fun.

As Glenelg was an open Park it did not have a face. While Luna Park

Left: Alfred Street gate, c. 1935; *below:* Back of face.

We looked for things that were bright at night time because night time was most of our business. We ducked away from dark greens and dark blues because they looked black at night. Everything was gaudy but tasteful.

– Ted Hopkins

The girls up in the offices had evening dresses on and they were all down at the front gate with the manager and all the crowd were lined up. There were thousands waiting to come in.

– Jack, Cabramatta

Luna Park was open and Sydney put on its old clothes and became young again.

– Sydney Morning Herald, *5 October 1935*

Brisbane had plans for a face, Luna Park at Scarborough Beach, Perth had a big black face with eyes looking at a large bee on its nose.

Luna Park Milsons Point opened to the public at 8 pm on 4 October 1935 – 8 Hour Day holiday weekend. That afternoon the Park had been officially opened by the Chief Secretary, Frank Chaffey, who took the place of the Deputy Premier, Michael Bruxner, who was ill. Also present were local aldermen and members of State Parliament. Outside 45 metre long queues waited in front of the face. An entrance fee of 6d for adults and 3d for children was charged and all rides were 6d except the Big Dipper and Coney Island which were 9d. (The entrance fee was abolished after the first year.)

From the opening of Luna Park, the face and towers were lit by coloured neon lights rented from Ray Neon. The installation was the largest in Australia. Three neon rings in the eyes flashed on and off to give the illusion of the eyes scanning from side to side and the eyebrows moving up and down. Laughter was broadcast from the base of the towers.

The fibro towers were decorated in the then popular art deco style. Original drawings show the masonry bases as "rock faced". The scalloping of the spires was inspired by New York's Chrysler Building which in 1930

Big Dipper, 1937.

My son cried after his first ride on the Big Dipper. He was only five. I thought the crying was in fear. But, as I found out from his first words after we alighted, he was disappointed at its conclusion.

– anon.

I believe that riding on the Big Dipper helped us as pilots in training for the war. The experience on the Dipper made it easier to confront flying.

– Jim, Turramurra

was the world's tallest building. The face was built from timber, chicken wire, canvas, plaster and paint.

The most popular ride was unquestionably the Big Dipper which made enough money on Saturday night to pay for all the other rides for the rest of the week. Once admitted to the Park, children screamed past other rides to queue up outside the Big Dipper. The ride lasted for three minutes and there could be up to three coaster carriages on the track at any one time travelling up to 80 kilometres an hour. You were raised 17 metres for a half mile ride. Until its demolition in 1981, the numbers on the various members from its dismantling in Glenelg and re-erection were still visible. A timber roller coaster was used instead of metal because it gave sway and movement in the track and a smoother ride.

The River Caves was the second most popular ride. The boats, original bridge (a showman's term for facade) and parts of the scenes came from Glenelg. A Japanese Tea Garden encased an extra 15 metres of channel. The southern supports of the Big Dipper penetrated the River Caves and part of the River Caves course went under the Big Dipper behind the Ghost Train. Spare boats were stored in a billabong against the cliff.

The Caves and their contents were constructed from horse hair and hessian dipped in plaster and draped over chicken wire. Items that had not come from Glenelg were built by sculptor Bim Hilder helped by Tommy Roberts and Michael Stoker. The mock sandstone was expertly applied by Mr Callagan who had searched the countryside for rock with suitable tones which he crushed and applied to wet cement. He even put cracks in. The glorious fake sandstone at Taronga Zoo, now almost all gone, was also his work.

The River Caves offered mystery and romance in dark low canals. The tranquil peace and quiet was a contrast to the noise and excitement outside. Escape was created through disorientation of space and time by a meandering stream through exotic scenes. While the Big Dipper attracted thrill seekers, the River Caves was a haven for romantics.

Rupert Browne's Ghost Train bridge connecting the Big Dipper Station and the River Caves was his greatest achievement. Although quite flat, the bridge had locomotives and mountains built in false perspective to give the illusion of depth.

Like the River Caves, the Ghost Train was a combined show and ride. Horror was achieved by loss of orientation amid surprise and fleeting glimpses of one's worst fears. Ultraviolet light on phosphorous paint created ghostly effects in the all-black interior. After the War, the Ghost Train carriages were replaced by round steel Twister cars (based on those at Tivoli Gardens in Copenhagen) which spun around when they struck a device on the floor. They were later prevented from spinning.

South of the River Caves was the Old Mill – a Dutch-style windmill whose only purpose was to attract attention to the point where the axis of the Midway shifted. Embellished with incandescent bulbs, the Windmill blades rotated. Underneath, Cahill's Restaurants ran a concession selling ice creams. This was later changed to the Chip Bar. Nearby was Let's Duk Sweetie.

Inside the Goofy House illusions such as the Magic Sword Illusion, the Galatea, the Girl's Head in the Miniature Bed and Sculptor's Dream were created by simple means.

Noah's Ark was a walk-through attraction with dark passages, gusty floors, sliding panels and humorous surprises in dioramas.

Between the Ark and the face was the Tumble Bug, a switchback railway imported from America which was first run by the Phillips across the road from Luna Park St Kilda, behind the Palais Theatre. The bridge to the Tumble Bug in Sydney was an enormous insect designed by Rupert Browne and built by Ted Hopkins. The eyes blinked and the nose slowly concertinaed back and forward.

At closing time, Coney Island was the first area to close. People often used their remaining tickets on the Tumble Bug on the way out.

The Penny Arcade was beyond the Big Dipper outside Coney Island. The facade and machines were brought from Glenelg. The original facade

Top: The Whirler, c. 1935; *above:* The Whip with Big Boys and the Whirler and Coney Island beyond.

My then boyfriend took me on the Big Dipper. Previously we'd had a Chinese meal and by the time the ride was finished I felt very queasy. We walked over to look at the pretty harbour lights and when he kissed me and asked me to marry him, I responded by throwing up all over him. Needless to say I never saw him after that night.

– Margaret, Cessnock

Luna Park sold the best hot chips in Sydney.

– Jennifer, Forestville

Changing bulbs on the onion dome on Coney Island, 1942.

I feel it is utterly necessary to create a world for children at heart and their children away from the painful realities of our world.
– Scott, Belrose

The River Caves contain some of the richest deposits of papier-mâché and plaster of Paris to be found in New South Wales
– A. Wit.

continued the Moorish style of the Big Dipper station. The extra arch added in Sydney was of a different architectural style. Slot machines offering fortune tellers, weight, strength, kickball, punchball, electric shock and "Pull the Tiger's Tail" machines gave cards with words of wisdom such as "Darling Boy: I'm sorry I turned you down for that other fellow; he is a rough-neck, and I love you only. Won't you please come back?" A palmistry machine dispensed a card after inserting a penny and putting your hand on a large brass hand. The flight path of an aeroplane could be manipulated. In exchange for a penny and your birth date, you would receive a horoscope card. Love, personality, the future, strength and skill could all be tested.

The culmination of the Midway was Coney Island – Funnyland, a simple human-scale amusement park within an amusement park. The Phillips and Abrahams could not agree on the name. To satisfy all parties, they called it both. The public knew it as Coney Island while staff referred to it as Funnyland. Stuart Bros are credited with the design and construction of Coney Island. Nevertheless, the initial decorative design was Rupert Browne's.

Original drawings show Coney Island painted in fake stone like the Giggle Palace at Luna Park St Kilda. Construction drawings named it the "Giggle Palace". The idea had come from similar funhouses in America and Europe where patrons participated as well as laughed at themselves and their fellow humans. Amusements and gadgets in Coney Island except the slot machines had been invented by American showman George Tilyou in his Pavilion of Fun.

Each facade of Coney Island was a different architectural style. Towards the railways, Coney Island's shed-like nature was fully revealed. The building was topped with a silver onion dome complete with flag pole. A ladder at the back gave access to the onion dome, where lights were changed by a man in a boatswain's chair on a rope off a pulley. One night an acrobat did a handstand on top of this dome. A staff member, Norm Bull, under the pseudonym Aldo the Great performed the Slide for Life. Holding a pulley in his teeth, he slid down a flying fox from the top of the dome to the Midway.

Inside Coney Island, amusements included the Joy Wheel, the Turkey Trot, slides, Barrels of Fun and distorting mirrors brought from England. The mechanical gadgetry for these had been fabricated at Luna Park St Kilda.

While Luna Park St Kilda's Giggle Palace had only a single barrel, Coney Island had two barrels revolving in opposite directions. The internal surface was polished floor boards.

Gravity down a slope was enjoyed on a simple mat on a slippery dip in contrast to the mechanical Big Dipper. When the steep northern slide known as the Devil's Drop was built in 1938 by Girvan Bros Builders to a profile the Phillips brothers had brought back from America, a portion of Coney Island's roof had to be raised. At that time the Barrels of Fun were moved to their present position.

Several devices on the entry walkway were removed due to accidents. The rope bridge under the slides was replaced with peep shows.

The work of Arthur Barton is most evident inside Coney Island. As a teenager he started a sign-writing company, Foxcroft and Barton, with the memorable motto: "Our Signs are Kneck Twisters". After active service in World War I, he studied art in England. Often described as Australia's Heath Robinson, Barton was a jack of all trades who, perhaps because his father was an engineer, had the ability to make his visions work and work simply. He wrote poems, illustrated books and cartoons, and was a quick sketch artist at David Jones; he also created the Christmas scenes in the windows of Farmers and Grace Bros department stores. He was probably drawn to Luna Park by his love of children. At Christmas he would lay out feasts for the local children on a table in his front garden under coloured festoon lights.

Barton started with Luna Park when it was being built. He and the painters who assisted him often reproduced images that the Phillips and David Atkins brought back from amusement parks overseas. He also depicted personalities from the Park and their expressions, such as Ted Hopkin's common saying, "You gotta laugh". The Ski Scene on Devil's Drop painted in 1970 has been described as his "Sistine Chapel" work. A notable

1935 view of Luna Park.

Luna Park was Sydney's heartbeat. Our fathers and mothers met at Luna Park. There was a ride called the River Caves in which they first kissed each other and when the children arrived they were brought there too.

– Clive James

Luna Park had its smells. There was always a smell of waffles, dampness and electricity. It was a wonderful mix. I noticed in Disneyland nothing smelt.

– Peter Kingston

Waltzing Dolls game in the Dodgem Building on the Midway.

When a good sort came along and went into the Caves by herself, I'd run along the side and jump in at the last minute. I missed once and ended up in the water.

–Tony, Belrose

I used to jump out of the boats in the River Caves and hide behind things and throw water at people. Sometimes we would pretend to be statues and watch people's faces as they tried to work out if we were real or part of the show. One time a door opened and a big bruiser grabbed me and my two mates. "Get in the next boat. I'll see you outside." We did and he took us aside. "You've got five minutes to be out of the park. If I see you after that I'll break your legs". His manner was quiet and carried great authority. Needless to say we left. We also never did it again.

–Philip, Lavender Bay

Someone bloody fired a bloody bloody decent sort of revolver in there [the Shooting Gallery] and bloody near blew a hole through the bloody half inch steel plate under the office.

– Dick Pearce

figure in the Park, Barton had a glass eye and wore a hat and bow tie with white overalls.

Coney Island was a treasure trove of Arthur Barton's murals. Above the windows facing the harbour was a long mural. The central section had a two-metre high version of the entry face and towers. This represented a simple pun: the original Luna Park was in Coney Island, New York; Luna Park, Sydney, contained Coney Island which in turn contained a miniature Luna Park.

High above the Turkey Trot, Barton created a huge animated diorama of the Early Bird Catches the Worm. Operated with crude but effective mechanics, a bird swooped down on a top-hatted worm whose body articulated up and down against a background of painted two-dimensional jungle scenes set in three-dimensional space.

From the exposed steel roof trusses hung metre-high painted canvas punkahs moved gently to circulate the air. Later a shooting game of monkeys climbing up and down in front of a jungle scene was located between the Turkey Trot and the slides. This was eventually replaced by Ray Guns, a light-operated shooting gallery built by Ted Hopkins.

Before the Midway awnings were built, people were allowed free admission to Coney Island on wet days.

Speedboat rides around Lavender Bay and out to the bridge were operated from the jetty off Coney Island by Fred Johnson as a concession.

To the right of the entrance to Coney Island was a milk bar which was run as a concession by Cahill's and to the left on the harbour was the Whirler. The Hey Dey, located to the south of the Whirler, was built in Australia to an American design. Four-seater cars with pivots on the front and two caster wheels spinning them in circles negotiated an oval track on a steel plate floor, making a hell of a racket.

A bandstand between the Hey Dey and the Dodgem Building held music recitals and bathing beauty contests. Uniformed brass band concerts were held free every Saturday night until 1956. Bands included the Water Board Band, the Northern Suburbs Brass Band, the New South Wales Railway Institute Band, the Police Band and the Tramways Band. In 1936 the Park was allowed to open on Sundays because it provided an afternoon band and an entry fee of a silver coin was charged.

The Dodgem Building was built partly on land and partly on the wharf left by Dorman Long. The facade of two-storey pointed arches was surmounted by a castellated parapet with shingled turrets and spires made from battened fibro which gave the impression of a stone castle.

Most of the interior was a full height space with a suspended electrified chicken-wire ceiling from which the dodgem cars ran. The dodgem cars were built in Melbourne. Two Auto Skooter cars (as well as the rights to reproduce them in Australia) were purchased by Leon Phillips from Lusse Bros in Philadelphia. Twenty-four were built in Melbourne to "Drive like fury – without a licence".

There was a Shooting Gallery at the southern end of the Dodgem building.

At ground level on the Midway was a variety of food and games – Oh You Cats (a ball throwing game), Box Ball, Waltzing Dolls (a roll down ball game), fairy floss and waffles, entrance to the Racing Dodgems, a milk bar and a dart game. The Phillips were not interested in running the games, so David Atkins ran them as a concession under his company David Atkins Pty Ltd which also had games at the Easter Show.

Later games were Spin It (bags of ball bearings thrown onto a plate that made it spin giving a score), the Bobs (a roll down game) and Hoopla. The Laughing Clowns replaced Spin It. Dick Pearce was sent to the Tivoli Theatre to see their laughing clowns. Jim Liston did the timber work while Dick fabricated the cast-iron components and put it all together. Initially the plaster heads were made by the manufacturers of the kewpies, Popeyes, kookaburras and sulphur-crested white cockatoos that were prizes. Sparrow Parsons ran the games.

Spiros Couttoupes made the waffles and fairy floss. The fairy floss came in a cone that was a white paper bag slit up one side. His father and uncle had brought the waffle recipe with them when they immigrated from Greece.

Top: Ghost Train; *above:* Ghost Train carriage, 1949.

The watchman, Bill Hibbert, on a number of occasions found someone locked in the Ghost Train overnight.

– Ronald, Bateau Bay

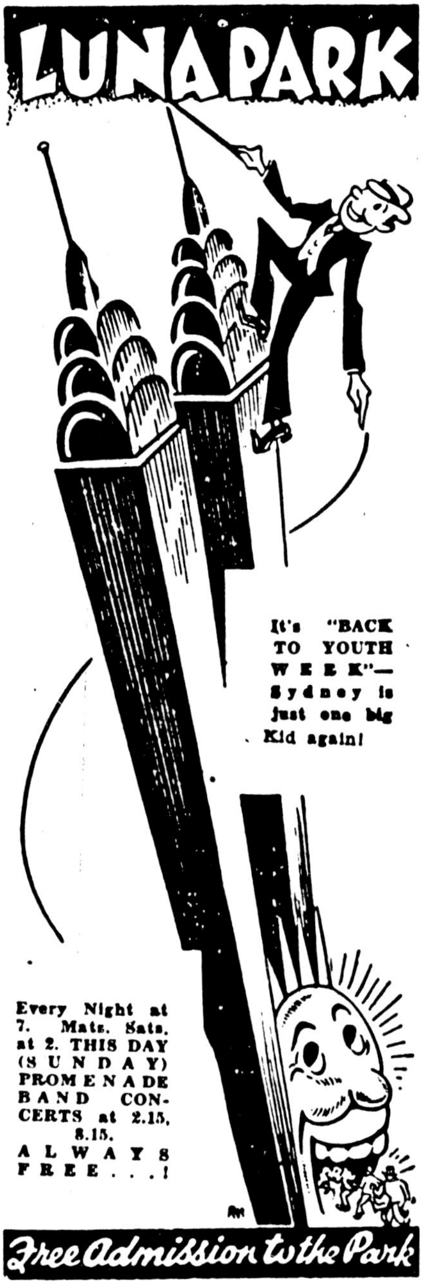

Opposite: 1935 panorama.

Above, on the southern harbour side in the Dodgem Building was a night watchman's flat (later used by the Phillips when they stayed in Sydney, then as store rooms and a recording room for the Park's tapes). North of this were the women's change rooms. In the centre of this area was a money counting room. The manager's office was on the Midway side with a commanding view up and down the Midway. Above his window were three big powerful coloured globes. Red meant "I want the patrolman quick"; green was for the maintenance fitter; yellow summoned the manager. Next to the manager's office were the accountant's office, the assistant manager's office, prize and costume stores and the men's change rooms to the north. The first aid room occupied the north-west corner at ground level.

On the Midway corner was a Photographic Studio where you could have your photograph taken with your head through holes in two-dimensional scenes: Batman and Robin, Tuxedo Man and a girl in a champagne glass, Luna Moon, a jail scene, a bar scene, a rural scene or even in a Goggomobile. A paper negative was used for speed. The studio was run by Harry Corbould and later by Cyril Brown whom David Atkins had tried to get removed from outside the face for taking photographs. As Council would not remove him, David Atkins asked "Would you rather be inside than outside?" and initially employed him to take shots on the Rotor. He later introduced instant photographic booths to the Park and Australia.

The Whip was south of the Dodgem Building. Like its equivalent in Luna Park St Kilda, the Whip came from the Coney Island New York workshops of its inventor, William F. Mangels. Tub-shaped cars, supported on a single pivoting arm, were carried about an oval track by a cable. On corners, the car suddenly spun out by centrifugal force. Two "Big Boy" sculptures turned around on revolving discs as the ride proceeded. TWURP TWURP was written round the neck of one of the sculptures, the other said BLEEP BLEEP. Similar sculptures existed on the Whip at Luna Park St Kilda.

The bridge to the Whip, a pelican, also incorporated the art deco inverted-dome motif of the Coney Island minarets. Live pelicans had always been a front-of-house attraction for menageries at English fairs as a symbol of luck.

South of the Whip was a carousel hired for the opening from showman Harry Stiller. A later carousel was rented from Alan Kale. These were the only rides not owned by Luna Park.

As the end of the night approached, Ted Hopkins, starting at Coney Island, would shine a torch at the cashiers as a signal for them to stop selling tickets and assemble their money. Similarly if David Atkins decided to close the Park due to rain, a few bars of "Land of Hope and Glory" would come over the loud speakers followed by – "Ladies and gentlemen, Mafeking has been relieved". (Mafeking was a besieged town in South Africa that was relieved during the Boer War by the British.) Later the broadcast signal was the lyrics "When day is done and shadows fall, I'll think of you..."

Luna Park and the North Sydney
Olympic Pool.

I was a single 24-year-old migrant living at Villawood Migrant Camp. In an attempt to meet an Australian female I went to the dance hall at Luna Park. I did get a dance or two but felt that the sheilas were rather snooty, so I caught the train back feeling rather lonely and dejected. The mention of Luna Park still evokes a certain feeling of sadness in me now.

– Otto, Warana

LUNA PARK MILSONS POINT

HEYDAY

After a very successful opening season, Luna Park closed for three months during the winter. This closure allowed the Park a breathing space for staff holidays and gave an opportunity to move, fully overhaul and paint rides, and introduce new attractions. Winter closures occurred until 1972.

At each season's opening, it was important for patrons to have the impression that everything was new or at least that things had changed. Before the opening of each season the foliage in the River Caves would be replaced with fresh clippings given by the Royal Botanical Gardens. The Phillips were not inclined to add new rides, so few were installed until the end of the war. Changes to the Park were mainly changes to the bridges.

A covered pontoon, the Floating Palais (later called the Palais de Danse), was moored off the Dodgem Building in 1936. This large flat concrete pontoon had a scissor-trussed roof supported by timber posts. Prior to Luna Park, ferries from Circular Quay dropped their passengers on this pontoon to either catch the train up the North Shore from the station (located approximately where Coney Island was later built) or to travel up Australia's first escalator to a tram stop in Glen Street. Luna Park rented the pontoon from the Department of Main Roads before purchasing it. Architect Samuel Lipson was employed to add a stage to the north of the pontoon, along with art deco rails, grilles with lights behind, lights and movable lattice screens to the harbour sides. Initially used for roller skating, it was transformed in 1939 to a dance hall because of the damage skates inflicted on the floor. Dances were held every Saturday night first to the music of Jim Coates and his Rhythm Boys and later Fred Switely and the Luna Park Band. People would come by ferry to Luna Park just for the dances.

Top: Fred Switeley (left) and the Luna Park Band in the Palais; *above:* Palais interior.

Right: Skee Roll; *below:* Sword swallower, Otto Baccus, swallowing a neon tube in the Mystic East.

All the people lined up outside. The first thing we would do before the park opened, a couple of minutes or two, we'd start that organ up and that brought the whole park to life with that atmosphere.

–Peter, Deepwater

The fire-eating bloke used to put a neon tube down, chin up, straight down, bare his chest and I'd have to switch it on. Bang the whole of his inside would light up. Every time I switched it on, I thought if this tube ever busts, I'll be up for manslaughter.

– Keith, Ermington

Opposite top: Charles Carmel carousel; *opposite bottom:* Carousel horse carved by Charles Carmel.

Arthur Barton later erected a waxworks in the Palais with exhibits such as a starving rat in a cage eating a man's belly. Members of the royal family and decorations used in the windows of Myers Melbourne to celebrate the coronation of Queen Elizabeth II were exhibited by Harold Spry as a concession. The waxworks was not a success and only lasted one season.

The Whip was not a popular ride and after the first season swapped positions with the Hey Dey, inheriting the pelican bridge. In 1940 the Whip was replaced by games and a glass blower who made human figures, ducks and swans. A roll down game called Skee Roll was added south of the Whirler. The Big Boy figures were moved to the entrance of Coney Island. Air rifles on the Parashoot shot at tin figures hanging from painted parachutes which spun around when hit. During the war, swastikas were painted on the figures. Kicking Mules, life-size mechanical mules, bucked boxes of chocolates back to the thrower if a ball hit the big bullseye on their bums. The skill was not only to hit the bullseye, but to catch the chocolates.

Herman Phillips bought a 1910 Charles Carmel American carousel in England and brought it to Sydney in about 20 marked pieces. Carmel was one of the great American carousel carvers in the first quarter of the century. Trusses supported a roof of coloured canvas above fretwork panels of foliage and mirrors – all surrounded by a frieze of paintings of exotic birds. Forty-three carved timber horses, a lion, a griffin and two chariots were driven by an electric motor. The outer ring of horses were more lavishly decorated with coloured saddlery and saddle cloths embellished with coloured jewels. The outside ring was fixed while the two inner rings moved up and down.

To make sure it worked, the carousel (called the Merry Go Round) was first assembled in the northern pylon of the Harbour Bridge. When installed

in Luna Park, it was located where previous carousels had been located. In 1938 it was slid on greased planks across to pride of place – immediately behind the face – to be the only ride on the Midway.

The Whirler bridge was moved down the Park as a bridge to the Milko game. Wooden balls were thrown at wooden milk bottles in front of an Arthur Barton mural of cows. This game was later replaced with the Bazookas which were balls fired by compressed air from a bazooka on a tripod at a jungle scene with Japanese soldiers poking their heads up out of a jungle of painted canvas fire hoses as vines.

The Midway was where it all happened. It was the street, the forum, the piazza, the stage, the audience. The Park had been laid out so that no attraction protruded into the Midway except the Windmill which marked the bend in the Midway. Pedestrian traffic tended to travel in a circle – along one side and back the other.

After one season it was decided to add canvas-covered awnings along the Midway to provide protection from summer rain. Although designed to be removable, once installed they were never taken down.

Sound was an integral part of Luna Park. At first the staff members such

Above: Bathing beauty contest; *right:* Speed boat ride from Coney Island jetty.

David Atkins had a mania for marches and circus music. I had every bloody march under the sun on seventy-eight records.
– Ted Hopkins

You don't want the music that loud so that you could tell a girl how beautiful she was without shouting in her ear.
– Ted Hopkins

as Keith Searle spruiked outside the attractions to draw people in. He dressed in an Indian outfit complete with turban to get people in to see Gogia Pasha – a fire-eater and magician from India. Live spruikers were replaced by tape recorders when they became available. Music was broadcast along the Midway initially from records and later tapes. In the 1970s Tom Jones endlessly sang *Delilah*.

The Luna Park song came from Luna Park St Kilda.

Take me out to Luna Park
Just for Fun
Where the lights shine after dark
Take me hon
The Crystal Maze I idolize
The Scenic's got me hypnotized
So take me out to Luna, dearie
Just for Fun. Fun.

– Words and music by Will H. Lewis

Special events were very much a part of Luna Park to entertain people on the Midway, especially as numbers thinned towards the end of the season. The opening season saw Uncle Luna's Water Pantomime, Uncle Luna and his Pantaluna Show, Uncle Luna's Harlequins, a Trambolina Act and a Jumble-Word Competition. On 31 January 1936 a group of Palm Island Aborigines who had starred in Charles Chauvel's film *The Uncivilised* were guests at Luna Park in full corroboree paint with spears, woomeras and boomerangs. In 1937 the Happy Hunter, a masked man in green hunting costume, roamed the grounds and gave free tickets to "the happiest people he can find".

As a publicity stunt in 1938, 10,000 Luna Park keys were dropped throughout Sydney's streets. Finders of the keys had the opportunity to try the lock on an oak treasure chest to win a £5 note. At the same time people were asked to "Greet lady tandem riders at Luna Park! These two game Westralian girls are on their last stage marathon tandem cycle ride Perth–Sydney!"

David Atkins claims he introduced carnival bathing-beauty competitions to Australia. From 1936 to 1942 a parade was held on the bandstand every year. Up to 300 entries of "sun-tanned redheads, brunettes and blondes" drew big crowds and received very good publicity. These contests were held over several weeks and culminated in the Grand Finale with prize presentation by some dignitary. A press photographer in May 1940 was quick to capture a photograph that made the front page of the *Daily News* of the winner, Betty Upton, planting a big kiss on the Mayor of North Sydney, John Cramer, as he presented her prize of £50.

For the 1936–37 season, a helium-filled captive advertising balloon was towed by a launch up and down Sydney Harbour.

Week-long Mardi Gras carnivals were held annually from 1936 to 1949. Huge inflated animals and figures were suspended 10 metres above the Midway as were boxes of confetti and balloons to be released randomly

Bigfella climb backwards chase wind away from me.

– Palm Island Aborigine commenting on the Big Dipper

Above: Charles Chauvel and the cast from the film *The Uncivilised; below:* Arthur Barton mural.

Right: Christmas decorations;
below: Escapologist.

One time they [Luna Park] let off their own fireworks and the whole lot went up at once as a spark got away.

– Harry Howard

I'd get a kid from the audience (200 people outside) and put him on the stage and make out I was hypnotising him and I'd put him in this box and I'd get these swords and put them through the box. I'd say to the kid before I put him in there, "You guide the swords through the holes". You'd put all the swords through and you'd swear all the swords were going through him. One bloody night the front of the bloody box blew open with the kid with all the swords around *him.*

– Keith, Ermington

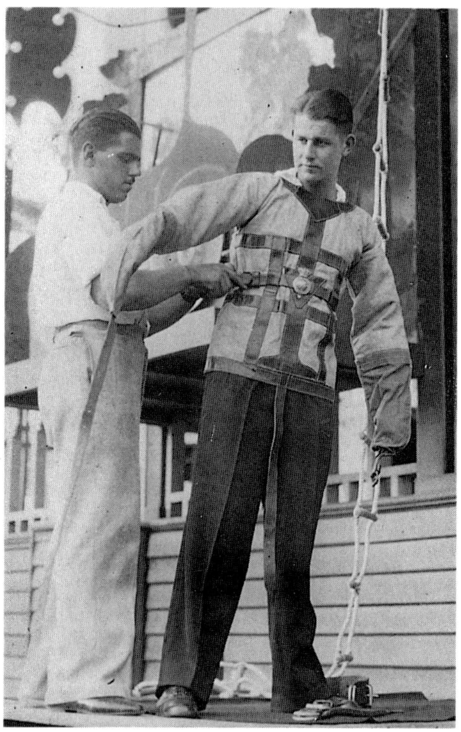

during the evening. The Midway was decorated with bunting, flags, pendants and Chinese lanterns. Luna Park staff wore huge masks and mingled with revellers in long twisting turning chains of people or in confetti battles.

New Year's Eve was a big event at Luna Park. Carnival hats and leis were sold on the Midway while Luna Park hosts and hostesses gave out free tickets for the rides. Usually the Park was comfortable at a crowd of six thousand and getting full at eight thousand. A crowd such as the fourteen thousand on New Year's Eve was unworkable. The Park was open all night with a fireworks display at midnight. Dancing started in the Palais at midnight.

Right from the opening season fireworks were a dynamic mid-air version of the way the Park's festooned lights decorated the night at ground level.

Night-time fireworks were set off from behind Coney Island usually by Howard and Sons. After the war, several surplus aircraft search lights scanned the night sky spotting gently-descending parachutes. A cliff-top display of a pyrotechnic clock with swinging pendulum was not a success as there was too much light from the Park.

Spectacular daytime fireworks bought from Japan were fired by mortar. At their zenith they exploded to open out as 6 metre diameter animals (such as elephants) made from tissue paper with their lower edges weighted so the animal itself formed the parachute.

The Midway attracted many unusual acts. In 1936 Gilbert, an escapologist in a straightjacket suspended by a burning rope attached to his ankles

above a flaming 44 gallon drum, "freed himself from the Gallows of Death". He was also a contortionist who could squeeze through an impossibly narrow brass keyhole.

The Flying Dunbars performed on a platform 10 metres above the Midway in 1939.

Bill and Ethel Woods had a display of tropical fish. Klimo the Clown rode the first smallest bike in the world. Mrs Cells and later her son, Jimmy, had performing monkeys, parrots and a couple of dogs. Jimmy also did tightrope walking on the Midway.

From the Bandstand seven-year-old Joy King would sing "I like aeroplane Jelly, Aeroplane Jelly for me..." to people who had cut a token from a jelly packet for free Aeroplane Jelly matinees boasting "Giant Aeroplane Jellies".

Gretna Green weddings were held outside the Shooting Gallery in 1936. Couples standing on either side of the anvil from the workshop received £50 to be married by the Park's blacksmith, Andy Anderson.

In 1936 the River Caves channel was partially dug up to increase the speed. A white mountain complete with operating "60 foot" waterfalls was added in August 1937 from a model built by Rupert Browne.

In 1938 the Spider was built locally by Nuttal Engineering from overseas plans. The bridge to the ride was a huge silver silastic spider with red head in a web of thick rope strung between two tree trunks. A maintenance fitter for Luna Park, Tom McCormack, had to have a steel plate inserted into his head after a Spider car spun around and struck him on the head.

Top: Boat coming out of the River Caves; *above:* River Caves.

Apart from Luna Park if we wanted to meet a better type of serviceman, we went to the Zoo; if we were looking for even better we went to the Museum.

– Yvonne, North Ryde

Someone that had dentures was sick on the Spider and chundered them. She got off and the attendant who had cleaned it up said to her 'I think these are yours'.
– Noeline, Matraville

A fella stood up and got chucked into the harbour and didn't get hurt. He was lucky.
– Ted Hopkins

Above: The Spider; *below:* Science Hall, 1938.

In the same year, a door maze was added to Noah's Ark – "it will confuse the mathematical brain of Einstein". A two-storey building was added to the front of the Goofy House in 1938 which was renamed Science Hall. The facade was a cubist face with entry through the mouth. Illusions were inside on the upper floor which was linked to the existing Goofy House. Exit was through the Mirror Maze which had been brought from Glenelg. This was a labyrinth of mirrors set between hexagonal posts and surrounded by holes emitting yellow fluorescent light.

When Science Hall was renamed the Hall of Science, a man with a black mortar-board and gown stood at the entry to collect tickets. The face was removed and replaced by laboratory imagery of retorts and test tubes beside the entry which was under a bowl of fire. Just inside the door was a mechanical magician made by Arthur Barton who would lift his hat up and then put it down again – each time revealing something different.

Changes to the Park's face were the result of the never-ending desire for novelty as well as its exposed aspect and construction of impermanent materials. The face erected in 1994 is the seventh expression. New expressions were literally applied over previous faces, with the different expressions probably modelled by either Rupert Browne or Arthur Barton. The first alteration was in 1939. Soon after only minor alterations were made with paint.

Before the war, David Atkins and Ted Hopkins went to Brisbane to investigate the possibility of setting up an amusement park. Nothing came of it, mainly because they felt the site was too hilly. T.H. Eslick, designer and builder of Luna Park St Kilda and White City in Sydney, left Australia in 1922 to construct theatres and amusement parks in America. He returned to design and construct Luna Park Brisbane at Breakfast Hill. A storm damaged the amusement section of the project which was never completed. Eslick disappeared shortly after Cloudland, Luna Park's Ballroom, was opened on 2 August 1940 and was never seen again. Another small Luna Park opened in August 1944 just outside Brisbane at Redcliffe.

From the beginning of the war in 1939, Luna Park's popularity flourished. Open seven days a week, it was a magnet for servicemen and their girls. Following Australia's declaration of war with Japan, the lights of Luna Park were "browned out" with shading on all visible external lights. The "brownout" only added to the romantic atmosphere of the Park. Neon lights were prohibited, so the face and other neons had to be turned off. To save power non-essential gimmicks, such as the workings of the Ghost Train bridge, were turned off .

Shirley Butler, a habitué of the Park, especially dances in the Palais, was last seen alive leaving Luna Park with a sailor on New Year's Eve. Her body was later found in Waverton.

During the war Luna Park was also frequented by prostitutes who would stand in the bright lights. They would be seen disappearing into the darkness under the Bridge with servicemen.

Top: Mannie McCarthy (left) and Leo Appo; *bottom:* Women woodchoppers, 1938.

One day a lady approached me and said "Why don't you have a section for us?" I thought it over and it seemed a good idea. So we had a ladies' woodchop. We had up to 50 competitors and they took it very seriously.

– David Atkins

One woman woodchopper cut her toe off one night.

– Eddie Devine

I was 15 the first time I won the woodchop at Luna Park. I won two years running – 1954 and 1955. The prize money was £20 for first place. I used a 5 1/2 pound axe and also hold the record fastest times – 8 inches in 35 seconds and later 10 inches in 32 seconds. I was Australian champion. I was made a life member of Metropolitan Sub Branch of Axemen's Association and also received the City of Wollongong Seal for bringing fame to the town.

– Jan, Wandandian

I went to Luna Park in 1941 aged 15 with my brother and met a soldier aged 22. I went there not intending to meet anyone. We went on many rides. I'm not sure whether I went home with my brother or not. I wrote to the soldier for some time. He was unfortunately killed in the war. It was a very romantic place.

– Merle

During the Second World War I used to dance in the Palais. A young English fellow who was on an aircraft carrier asked me to dance. He was twenty and I was eighteen years of age. We were married the following year after he was discharged in Australia at the end of the war.

– Enid, Ryde

I've seen that area from the carousel to the front gate one seething mass of brawling servicemen during the war. It was usually Americans versus Australians.

– Peter, Beacon Hill

If ever there was a fight with sailors she'd be mixed up with it.

– Ronald, Bateau Bay

You couldn't get in there. It was because of servicemen and people didn't give a damn about money. the war's here, the Japanese were bombing Darwin – let's get rid of it. the girls were happy to make servicemen spend. They all had money.

– Cyril, Sans Souci

When my uncle came home during the war for R & R, he went to Luna Park with my father, had a few beers and swam from Luna Park to the south side.

– Jennifer

Face, c. 1938.

We had some terrible faces. It took us years to get a good face. Years to get the face we wanted. They played around with it and played round with it.

– Ted Hopkins

Left: Face, c. 1950; *below:* Ferry to Luna Park; *bottom:* Entrance face to Luna Park Scarborough Beach, Western Australia.

One year I asked my father why we always went to Luna Park to see Santa. Why couldn't we go to the North Pole to visit him? My father replied that Santa had moved his home to Luna Park as it was a nicer place to live than the very cold North Pole. He also said when the children came to visit him at Luna Park, they could have fun on all the rides. My father said that Santa loved to see and hear children smile and laugh, that's why Luna Park had a big face laughing out the front.

– Julliet, Nundah

Right: Oriental Entertainer somersaulting with cup and saucer on tray; *below:* Mystic East; *bottom:* Spider Woman illusion.

Luna Park lived up to its motto: Just for Fun.
–Tony, Carringbah

Tom McCormack, fitter, in front of mannequins who were having their photos taken for a magazine, was going to put on a bit of an act for them. He was going to come down standing up on the mat instead of sitting on it. Tom goes up all right and comes hurtling down to draw a bit of attention to himself. When the mat hit the cross ones he just flew straight off the mat straight onto the concrete on his face in front of them.
– Les, Sans Souci

I remember him telling us that he was fed up with the other men helping themselves to his cigarettes. He did what any good snake charmer would do – he put the largest snake he could fit into his coat pocket so when the hand went in to take the cigarettes…horror or horrors, the snake. From then on, no missing cigarettes.
– Jean, Bronte Beach

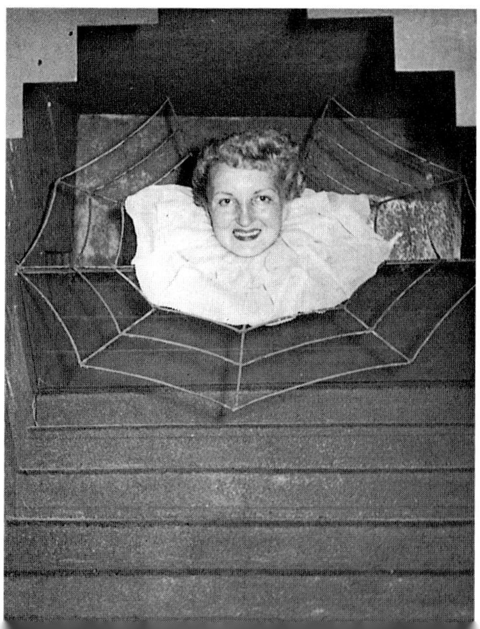

Plans to use Luna Park for military storage purposes were considered shortly after the "brownout". These were never implemented as the railway was a bottleneck and the site was too close to the Bridge. David Atkins argued the importance of the role the Park played for recreation for both citizens and servicemen.

An air raid shelter was cut by staff into the cliff immediately behind the Ghost Train; it was only used once when the Japanese submarines entered Sydney Harbour.

In September 1940 the Parashoot was replaced by the Mystic East – an authentic Burmese pavilion carved in Burma. In 1924 it had been the Burmese Pavilion at the British Empire Exhibition at Wembley. The pavilion and contents were then brought to Australia for exhibition at the Royal Easter Show as the Schweppes refreshment pavilion. When the military took over the Showground during the war, the pavilion and contents were bought by showman, Stan Durkin, who sold them to Luna Park. A special shed built for these Burmese treasures was erected north of the bandstand. Inside there was a white marble and gold Buddha, a life-size carved beggar, a Burmese prayer bell and Burmese ornamentations. An attendant lectured on Burmese architecture. During one season a troupe of Chinese acrobats called Oriental Entertainers performed double somersaults holding a tray of crockery without breaking a piece, fire eating, contortions, diving through a circle of knives and spinning plates on sticks. They lived behind the Mystic East during their stay.

Illusions such as the Spider Woman, the Galatea, the Girl on the Swing and the Girl in the Coffin were also presented in the Mystic East. The Spider Woman was a girl's head in the centre of a spider's web. She appeared to not have a body. The Girl in the Swing was similar but she was on a swing with her arms holding the ropes of the swing. The Galatea was a girl who changed to a skeleton, then to a bunch of flowers. A magician hypnotised a girl in a coffin, then made her rise up out of the coffin. A hoop was run over the body to assure viewers that there were no strings.

Shah Nazir from India, performed tricks with snakes. A sword swallower, Otto Baccus, wired up neon tubes and stuck them down his throat – all 10,000 volts.

In 1943 the Mystic East facade was removed, stored on top of the cliff and replaced by Model Electric City. The prayer bell was stored in Coney Island while the Buddha and some embellishments were installed in the River Caves in the Japanese tea garden scene. Due to the war, the scene was changed from Japanese to Burmese with sound effects of cymbals from the *The King and I* added later. Buddha presided over the endless river.

The Model Electric City was a large miniature landscape of Hornby trains in action. Ted Hopkins calculated that the distance travelled by the trains in a week was equivalent to the train trip from Sydney to Melbourne and back. This was removed before the end of the war.

WEDNESDAY, DAILY TELEGRAPH DECEMBER 5, 1945 3

ACCUSES NAZIS

PRINCE AT LUNA PARK

PRINCE PHILIP OF GREECE (foreground), cousin of Princess Marina, second cousin of King George, taking a tumble in the revolving barrel at Luna Park last night. With fellow-officers of the Royal Navy destroyer H.M.S. Whelp, on which he is a lieutenant, Prince Philip visited Luna Park after a farewell party aboard the ship last night.

TIDAL WAVE KILLS 4000, WRECKS VILLAGES

Daily Telegraph Service and A.A.P.

LONDON, Tuesday.—A tidal wave which struck a 100-mile coastal belt west of Karachi (north-west India) last Wednesday, is believed to have killed 4000

Germans Resent U.S. Occupation

Daily Telegraph Service

NEW YORK, Tuesday. — German resentment over U.S. occupation

Above: Daily Telegraph, 5 December 1945; *below:* Snake charmer, 1940.

A submarine came in during the war. The shelter was chock-a-block with staff and the rest of them. I had to wait outside.

– *Ted Hopkins*

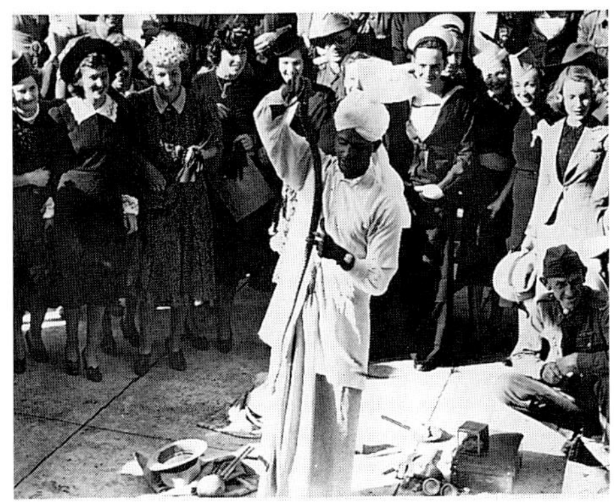

Tumble Bug.

It was always a pretty good mixture.
You know, the average working class.
– George, Ermington

In November 1945 an obsolete submarine with K12 painted on its side was acquired from the Dutch Navy. It was moored off Coney Island for exhibition. Owned by a syndicate including Ted Hopkins and David Atkins, it was run at Luna Park as a concession with an admission charge. Big holes were cut in its deck towards the bow and stern to let people in. Stairs were added as well as guard rails through the whole interior which was complete with tools, manuals and charts.

After the war when Sydney was plagued with power shortages and restrictions, the K12 was used as a booster to the Park's electricity supply. Its batteries would be charged during the day to light the Park at night. Although obsolete, it still had one engine with generators and batteries operable. By 1948 its usefulness had diminished and it was moved to Manly

Pier where it was again moored as an attraction. During a storm, it broke free and drifted to Middle Head where it ran aground and was towed to Kerosene Bay near Balls Head where it was left to rust.

On 26 April 1946, a 33-year-old New Caledonian crewman, Frederick Chitty, disregarded warning signs and sat on the side of a Big Dipper carriage. He overbalanced on a curve, was thrown against a pole and was killed.

Money became tight and materials scarce and expensive after the war. When the neon lights of the face were again turned on, most of them were faulty. Although repairs were carried out, they caused a fire in April 1947 which destroyed the scalloped spire of the south-west tower. The automatic fire sprinklers were of no use as they were fitted to the interior of the tower. Fearing another more devastating fire, the neon lights were replaced with incandescent bulbs. Shortly after this the facial expression was again altered to one of its worst, that of a clumsy mutilated expression.

Top: Big Dipper; *above:* Bar scene in Photographic Studio, 1936.

Above: Interior of Coney Island with slides; *right:* Laughing Clowns.

The worst splinter I've ever had in my life was from the slides. I'll never forget it. I can see it now. It stayed with me for months. You accepted that and didn't go and sue anyone in those days.

Peter Kingston

The big spider on the bottom of the Crazy House was always very impressive when you were a mere six year old

– Jan, Kiama

Dick Pearce, who worked on the maintenance of Luna Park from 1935 to 1980, recalls that the face was remodelled many times because it was very slowly sagging which caused it to crack and break up. Extra internal support was added to compensate for the weight of extra plaster added with each facelift. He estimated the distance from the teeth to the ground had decreased by 600 mm over the years.

Following a dispute with the Phillips, David Atkins resigned as manager although he retained the games concession. The new manager, Mr Haynes replaced Duk Sweetie with the Jack and Jill. Built on site to plans from Luna Park St Kilda, it was similar to Frederic Thompson's Human Toboggan Slide in Luna Park Coney Island. Patrons were transported in bucket-like seats to the top of the cliff where they were tipped out sideways to slide down a "U" shaped slide on a mat. The ride was not very popular, no doubt due to the many accidents that occurred on it. Elbows were often burned by friction with the slide. It only lasted three to four years.

On the Midway in front of the Jack and Jill, Murray the Escapologist in a sweeping cape was put in a straightjacket and placed in a box secured by chains that was lowered into a large tank of water. When the tarpaulin covering the tank was removed, he was out and alive.

After twelve months David Atkins was reinstated as manager.

In about 1947 a Crazy House (also known as the House Upside Down or Topsy Turvy) was added north of the Hall of Science. People sat back to back on a swinging seat in a room decorated as a wallpapered domestic interior complete with curtains, pictures on the walls, cupboards and a big old radio. Attendants gave the seat a push to start the illusion. The surrounding room was then rotated: your eyes told your brain that you were swinging head over heels. If you closed your eyes your balance told you that you were simply sitting on a seat. It was not very successful as it was not a repeat ride.

Under the southern end of the Dodgem Building, Arthur Barton and Nat Baggs built and operated as a concession a simulated ride in a submarine (much like Frederic Thompson's A Trip to the Moon at Luna Park Coney Island and Luna Park St Kilda's Train Crash). Once people were inside, water would rise between two panes of glass as scenes moved outside, giving the impression the submarine was diving as the interior rocked gently. A tape recorder provided appropriate sound effects.

In about 1948 David Atkins purchased a mechanical realistic life-size elephant complete with elephant sounds. A driver dressed as a rajah operated levers behind its head while three people could sit on either side on top while it walked along the Midway. The elephant only lasted one season due to mechanical problems and the novelty soon wore off.

In 1949 a Rock-o-Plane, a type of Ferris Wheel with wire-enclosed cages, was added. A handle inside the cage allowed the occupants to choose whether they were turned completely head-over-heels or not. This ride was run as a concession by Larry Quillen who had the ride made in

Above: Slides in Coney Island; *below:* Postcard from Photographic Studio.

Twinkle Twinkle, Luna lights
Come across, and see the sights
Enjoy yourself – admission's free
The gang's all here – or ought to be!
– *1937 ad*

Australia from overseas plans. Luna Park later bought the ride. After 1970 it was moved to the cliff top as an advertisement.

A new Penny Arcade building with curved-top beams painted with Wild West scenes by Arthur Barton was added to the south end of the Dodgem Building. Outside was a giant 1949 (and later 1959) coin. A shooting gallery was inside with the arcade machines. The .22 rifles were stored in a rack in the main office each night. They were restricted to limited swing after an attendant getting them from the storage rack was shot in the stomach and died.

Night-time view of Luna Park and North Sydney Olympic Pool.

LUNA PARK MILSONS POINT

A CHANGE OF OWNERSHIP

In 1950, David Atkins (on behalf of a group consisting of Dr H.G. (Doc) Harding, Jock McLaughlan, Ted Hopkins and himself) bought out the shares of Leon and Harold Phillips who were then in their mid-sixties. By this time the Park was desperately in need of new equipment. In 1951 David Atkins and Ted Hopkins went on a world tour and bought the U-Drive, Flying Saucer, new dodgem cars and several new slot machines.

The Flying Saucer was purchased in Utrecht, Holland, to replace the Hey Dey. In Sydney scenery of a big city was added around the circumference and was painted on the edge of the central disc which spun in the opposite direction to give the illusion of speeding through a city in a flying saucer. The central disc at one time had a human head at its centre and later a standing superman. The bridge was Pop-eye riding a rocket.

The U-Drive replaced the Whirler and adopted the pelican bridge. Ted Hopkins built the electrified track for the imported cars. Faster than the Dodgems, the U-Drive was the most popular ride after the Big Dipper and Coney Island and on par with the River Caves.

Also in 1950 an American servicemen, S. John Ross, joined Luna Park. He was a silhouette artist whose stall was just north of the Windmill. Born in Detroit, he spent five hours at the age of twelve watching Bud-Jack (acclaimed as the greatest silhouette artist in the world) at the Michigan State Fair. Later he met Bud-Jack who taught him the art of silhouette cutting as well as sending him to art school. S. John Ross came to Australia in 1942 and was selected to set up General Douglas MacArthur's office in Sydney. After fighting in the Philippines, he returned to Sydney after the war to cut silhouettes at shows. Cutting the silhouettes was only part of the

Queues waiting for the gates to open

Luna Park was a fantastic land where you could be anyone you wanted – especially with those mirrors.

– Philippa

Above: Cut-out silhouette of Ted Hopkins by S. John Ross; *right:* S. John Ross (right) cutting the silhouette of Little Patti with Col Joye.

Many Aussies have been preserved by me.
– *S. John Ross*

You're the man that separates black from white.
– *Martin Sharp*

When you cut out a person's profile you learn more about them than the skin and bones which make up the face. You find out what sort of people they are. I try to translate that to paper.
– *S. John Ross*

attraction: S. John Ross' warm outgoing personality charmed and amused his subjects as well as onlookers.

The Hall of Science facade and name were replaced in 1950 by Davy Jones Locker, an idea borrowed from Rockaway's Playland amusement park in New York. The facade was recreated by Arthur Barton with glass panels in front of a man in a deep sea diving suit, a mermaid whose tail moved, and fish. Bubbles coming up the glass gave the illusion of being underwater. Inside above the front were distorting mirrors and Arthur Barton cartoons. One of the illusions was underwater canaries: inside a big water-filled glass bowl was another bowl with canaries in it, giving the illusion that the canaries were under water.

Behind this was Davy Jones Locker itself – the former tilted room of the Goofy House was lined with fish aquariums to give the impression of a ship's interior on the sea bed. Just before the Mirror Maze exit was the Watering Boy diorama – when you looked through a window at a scene of a boy watering a garden, he squirted you in the face. In a similar way, as you approached the three ring circus and stepped on a mat, the light would go on and the elephant would squirt water on the glass at you.

On the roof of the ticket box Arthur Barton created a life-size dummy who looked like Oliver Hardy complete with bowler hat and a walking stick called Talking Charlie. This was Luna Park's brave attempt at animatronics as a tape recorded voice spruiked out of a moving rubberised mouth.

Left: Davy Jones Locker; *above:* Davy Jones Locker at Rockaway, New York.

A new entry was added to Noah's Ark. This was a copy of a similar entry in Pleasure Beach, Blackpool, recreated by Arthur Barton and built by Harry Holland. The entry was decorated with large sunflowers. On the roof were enormous cut-outs: a rhinoceros, kangaroo, dinosaur, Noah, a dog and a man in military uniform.

David Atkins travelled to Germany to see a new amusement device that was drawing huge crowds there. The Rotor, designed by Ernst Hoffmeister, was first shown at the Munich Festival in October 1949. Patent rights for the Rotor were secured by David Atkins and Ted Hopkins after seeing a Rotor at the Festival of Britain in 1951.

The patent purchased from Hoffmeister merely consisted of the diameter of the drum, its speed and the co-efficient of friction of the rubber that lined its walls. The rest was improvised by Ted Hopkins. The drum revolved at 30 revolutions per minute, delivering a 1–1.5 g force: enough to stick someone to the wall and not let them slide down. Three Rotors were built: one for Milsons Point, one for St Kilda and the third was destroyed by fire while being transported to the Brisbane Show.

In October 1951, at a cost of £12,000, the Rotor replaced the bandstand. After paying the entry fee, a passage wound around the drum, forming a spiral down to where at the last minute you could choose to participate or just watch.

Staff would stage stunts on the Rotor such as setting up a card table with two chairs and playing cards. Keith Searle suspended a girl horizontally

I found with the running of Luna Park, that a show like Davy Jones Locker and Science Hall took a certain class of people. When they disappeared there was nothing. They missed them.

– Ted Hopkins

The true heart of Luna Park lay in illusion. The World of the Impossible. Even at the age of twelve you know, you absolutely know, that water cannot run uphill and bowling balls do not defy the force of gravity. But they did in Davy Jones Locker. Oh yes, you could stand there and realise that the whole of Davy Jones Locker was built on an angle and that the bowling balls that ran uphill and the water flowing upwards was actually on a slight decline. But intelligence be buggered. Your senses still told you they were running uphill. I remember thinking as a child that when there is a battle between knowledge and sensation, sensation always wins. In a modified way, this has become the basis of my adult business life.

– Bill, Bilgola

As a three-year-old, I ran away from home only to be apprehended in the Mirror Maze by a policeman and taken home on the back of his bike.

– Peter, Lane Cove

People would throw up on the Rotor as it was spinning. What a sight! The vomit would project outwards for a second and then head straight back at high speed.
– Owen, Rosebank

The vomit was also subject to this gravity-defying feat and would travel from the mouth of the sick kid along the rubber wall. You could see it coming but there was nothing you could do to get out of the way.
– Susan, Surry Hills

Opposite: In the Rotor; *right:* Keith Searle in the Rotor; *below:* Rotor facade, 1973.

I remember sliding down with my dress sliding up revealing iridescent green knickers with a heart and "I Love You" in the centre. The attendant said I could have another go for free.
– Doreen, Canberra

One night a woman on it split her underpants and there was a big crowd and they were cheering her. The lights were strong so you couldn't miss a trick. After the ride had stopped she got out in the middle of the floor pulled up her dress, completely nude, and said "Now have a bloody good look".
– Keith, Ermington

It was fun to see them go up and down. Women would come down and their dresses would come up and the crowd would roar like buggery.
– Ted Hopkins

Johnnie Ray was there one night. He had a big crowd with him. They put him on the Rotor. I started 'er up, spinning 'er around and dropped the floor. I thought he was going to piss himself. They screamed out "Stop the Rotor" and they practically had to carry him off.
– Keith, Ermington

It took us years to get a satisfactory face. It's not an easy job on that size to get exactly what we wanted, a welcoming Father Christmas face.

– Ted Hopkins

Right: Arthur Barton with schoolboys painting clown face, 1950; *below:* Remodelling of Arthur Barton face, 1953.

Being squashed till you wanted to be sick on the Cha Cha, laughing till you wet your pants.

– Julie, Ainslie

with a rope held in his teeth. Alan Nye was the first person in Australia to walk the wall. He refused an offer to make a lot of money in America from an amusement park operator who claimed that Alan was first in the world to walk on wall. Cyril Brown from the Photographic Studio would photograph people on the Rotor then give them a ticket for the photo as they got off.

Designs for the Cha-Cha (a Scrambler designed by the Eli Bridge Company) were bought in America and built in Australia by Nuttal Engineering. The sensation of speed was doubled as each counter-clockwise turning car flashed by a car swinging clockwise. The Cha Cha replaced the Jack and Jill next to the Crazy House and "took good money".

In the late 1950s the face was again remodelled. Arthur Barton modelled

a meter-high maquette which was then translated to full size. This face is commonly referred to as the Arthur Barton face, that of Old King Cole (for he was a merry old soul) and without doubt was the most popular expression as it was charged with emotion – beaming with happiness and on the verge of breaking out into raucous laughter.

Luna Park attracted an unusual range of people as staff. The full-time day staff who maintained the Park during the day and the closed winter period were fitters, electricians and painters. Dedicated men such as Dick Pearce, Eddie Devine, Arthur Barton and later Tony Maloney spent most of their working lives maintaining Luna Park.

Harry Holland was a member of the day staff who was a world famous motorbike rider on the Wall of Death (a cylinder). He came from England

Left: Arthur Barton face, c. 1953; *below:* Palmistry game.

The staff were not unionised as they would get a better deal from me than the unions.
– Ted Hopkins

You'd have to commit a murder before he'd get rid of you.
– Anon.

Any success that I had at Luna Park was due to the staff I had around me.
– Ted Hopkins

Harry Holland was a star, the best in the world, finished up shootin' himself in a room living on his own.
– Jack, Cabramatta

Midway looking toward Coney Island.

Redcoats caused a lot of the fights. A lot of them were ex-boxers and fancied themselves.

– Noeline, Matraville

with his 1925 red and cream Indian Scout motorcycle in about 1948, but the Wall of Death never operated at Luna Park. He also had an Austin 7 with a platform for a lion to stand on as part of the act.

Most night staff had a daytime job outside Luna Park. Luna Park gave them the opportunity to earn extra money to pay off houses, cars, etc. The bouncers for the Park, named Redcoats because of the coats they wore, were usually ex-boxers and ex-wrestlers. Fights sometimes broke out at the face as the Redcoats would not admit anyone under the influence of alcohol. All parcels suspected of containing liquor were checked at the gate.

David Atkins ("DA") and especially Ted Hopkins ("Hoppy") were a team who commanded the respect of their staff.

David Atkins was a true showman, one of the best in Australia, with the personality to match it. He understood how to get people in and what they wanted. He had the ideas – "I've got enough stored up in my mind to keep us going for another 20 years". Married to Alva, the daughter of George Green (one of New Zealand's best known showmen), he was also a keen gambler who participated in speculative ventures such as a gold mine in New Guinea. He could not resist a bargain – buying up army surplus and cheap Japanese stock to use as throwaways at his games so no one went away without a prize. He was very generous.

Ted Hopkins made things happen – supervising the construction and maintenance of rides. He was very much a hands-on boss. When the Park was open he walked around it every couple of hours, often striding down the Midway dressed in a suit with a spanner in one hand and a grease gun in the other, followed by a team of men in blue overalls to fix a ride. He was the first up the ladder or under a ride. Arriving at work at 8.00 am, he did not leave until 11.45 pm. At the beginning of the season, the Big Dipper car was sent around the track by itself, then Ted Hopkins would ride it to ensure its safety for the public. He also was the first to ride it before every session.

The door of Ted Hopkins' office was always open for staff to settle any grievances. When a staff member played up, Ted Hopkins would say "I don't blame you, I blame myself for trusting you". When staff grew old they were not sacked but simply moved to a different job.

Following an overseas trip, David Atkins brought three spectacular acts to Luna Park in 1953. Mike Berosini, "The Great Berosini – The Daredevil of the Wire -- Stratosphere Man" from Palisades Park, New York performed on a 25-metre high swaypole to the sound of *April in Paris*. When he performed, the adjacent rides (U-Drive and Big Dipper), were stopped and their lights turned out. Half way up the pole was a horizontal outrigger that the blindfolded Berosini would walk out on. He would put his foot over the end as if he were going to walk right off. He also rode a bicycle out the outrigger. Then he went up the swaypole and did handstands on top while

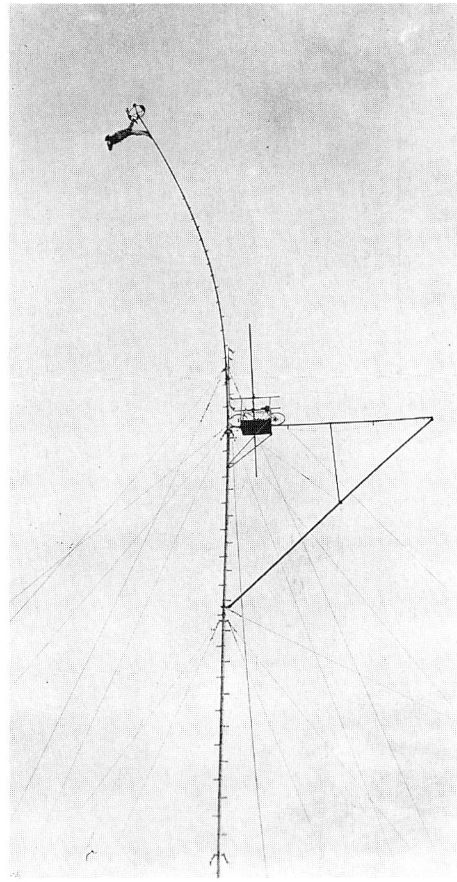

The Great Berosini.

This was probably the best one man act ever presented in Australia.
– Ted Hopkins

But Hopkins, Jesus, he could do anything. He was a rigger, he could tie knots, he could weld, he could do anything. God, he was a clever man, he could rewind a motor. And on the side he was a photographer, a genius of a photographer. He could do anything.
– Jack, Cabramatta

Above: Don Webb, diver; *right:* Ball game; *below:* Dixie Lee's high ladder act.

Years later Webb died. He missed.
– Ken, Woolloomoolloo

the pole swayed from side to side. He finished balancing on one hand, taking his hat off to the crowd with the other.

Don Webb, from Toronto, dived 12 metres into a 2.1 metre deep tank of water. At the last minute he crouched into a ball so his legs took the impact.

Dixie Lee (Bell) from Dayton, Ohio, who had performed 12 metres above Madison Square Garden as well as with the Ringling Bros, performed her high ladder act, spinning on a rope held only in her teeth. She retired from show business after her appearances at Luna Park.

Events impressive as these were not continued. They were expensive and people would crowd the Midway to watch, instead of paying to go on the rides.

Men's and women's woodchopping and sawing contests were held behind the face and later in front of the Big Dipper station until 1959. Mannie McCarthy (world champion underhand axeman) competed against champion Leo Appo.

David Atkins and Ted Hopkins were committed to helping the underprivileged. For one day each year the Park was opened free for the children of the Far West Children's Home, the Sunshine Home, the Spastic Centre and orphanages. Luna Park contributed a bag of chips, a bag of lollies and an ice cream.

For a month in 1956, scenes for the movie *The Summer of the Seventeenth Doll* were shot in the Park. Stars in the movie included Ernest Borgnine, Anne Baxter, Angela Lansbury and John Mills. For the movie, the

sign for the River Caves was substituted with a "Tunnel of Love" sign. The front of Penny Arcade was used for the boxing scene although the interior scenes were shot later in the studio.

ROO: I'll tell you what, let's go down to Luna Park and celebrate eh?
OLIVE: Nobody cares.
ROO: Orr sure they do. It's just sitting around here that's doing us in, that's all. Come on, we'll make a real night of it all eh?

– *Summer of the Seventeenth Doll* film script

Luna Park always attracted visiting and local celebrities. In 1936 world-renowned contralto, Miss Eileen Boyd sang and middle-weight champion boxer Fred Henneberry gave a boxing display on a specially erected stage. In December 1945, Prince Phillip of Greece (now the Duke of Edinburgh) was escorted out of the River Caves for getting out of his boat. Other well-known visitors included Bea Miles, Penny Jack, Smokey Dawson and horse, Vic Damone, Rosaleen Norton, Abe Saffron, Johnnie Ray, Johnny Farnham, Little Patti, Col Joye, John Meillon, Connie Francis, Barry Humphries, Alfred Hitchcock, Violet Carsons from *Coronation Street*, Brett Whiteley, Robert Hughes, Jack Davey, cyclist Hubert Opperman and the Harlem Globe Trotters. Sequences for TV programs such as Johnny O'Keefe's *Six o'clock Rock* and *Skippy* were shot at Luna Park. In 1969 Miss Australia contestants visited the Park. On 12 January 1979 Tiny Tim set a new world non-stop professional singing record of 2 hours 15 minutes in the Palais.

Left: Scenes on the U Drive from *Skippy; above:* Johnnie Ray on the Spider; *below:* Filming *The Summer of the Seventeenth Doll*

Johnnie Ray was there. All the girls were hanging off him and tearing his clothes off.

– S. John Ross

I should like another ride on the Big Dipper. You all think, I suppose, that I am used to thrills, but I think it is much more thrilling than flying.

– Jean Batten, aviatrix

Above: Flying Saucer, 1956; *right:* Flying Saucer and Superman.

When clutching my six-year-old son on the Flying Saucer and assuring him that all was safe, there came a muffled bleat , "Mum, you're strangling me!".

– Rosemary, Hunters Hill

A day at Luna Park was better than 10 trips to the Easter Show.

– Anon

I rang up the builder in England asking how much he wanted for the plans. Five hundred quid. I'll see you next week. That was Thursday...I was there on the Monday. Do it now, there might be a law against it tomorrow.

– Ted Hopkins

David Atkins died suddenly from a heart attack in 1957. Ted Hopkins became manager with Doc Harding as chairman of directors.

In 1959 Luna Park became responsible to the Department of Labour and Industry for its safety standards. No suggestions were made for any improvements to safety standards already carried out by the Park.

Ted Hopkins bought an old Motor Cycle Speedway ride. Motor bikes four abreast roared around an undulating track.

Plans for the Calypso were bought in 1961 from Battersea Park in England. The ride was built locally and replaced the Motor Cycle Speedway immediately behind the face on the harbour side. Cars spun on a platform that spun – all of which could be tilted up. The operator could manipulate each of these movements. The Calypso was transported to the Showground for the Easter Show, where it was the first new ride since the war.

The Calypso and what remained of the Mystic East were destroyed by a fire on top of the cliff where they were being stored.

Ted Hopkins saw the Wild Mouse in America in 1958 and made tentative arrangements to buy the plans. In 1962 he and Dick Pearce travelled

Left: Boys from the Far West Children's Home on the Wild Mouse; *below:* Ted Hopkins (left) and Dick Pearce with the Wild Mouse car from America.

My sister told me two things: 1) If you go on the front of the Big Dipper it's less scary than the back and 2) the Wild Mouse is not as scary as the Big Dipper. I never trusted her again.

– anon.

The art of operating the Mouse was splitting up two good looking girls so you could jump in with one of them to chat 'em up.

– Tony, Belrose

to the Seattle World Trade Fair to buy the plans and observe its operation. They brought back a car to be copied locally.

Three Wild Mouse tracks were built – Luna Park Milsons Point (also used at the Sydney Showground) and Melbourne and Perth Showgrounds. The Wild Mouse was the first roller coaster at the Sydney Showground.

Underneath the Wild Mouse slab was a large pond for the Skooter Boats. These were small boats with propellers that could be turned through 360°. Power delivery was similar to the Dodgems except the steel plate floor was Sydney Harbour salt water with copper electrodes in it. Driving instructions would come over loud speaker: "This is your captain speaking…".

At ground level on the Midway were two ball games – on the northern corner was Bathing Beauties and then the Basket Ball game. Bathing Beauties were bathing costume clad shop mannequins with one moveable

We had a birthday party there, many years ago. The birthday boy is 40 now. He had rides in everything , with his guests. The favourite was the something mouse. After the first ride on it he was green!! I expected him to groan "Let's go home" or "I am going to be sick", but he said "I'm going on it again!"

– anon.

The Wild Mouse whipped out into the night at hair raising speeds scaring us kids half to death.

– Anon.

Right: Air gust and padded ball in Coney Island; *below:* Mayhem as the gates are opened.

After 1960 rides became so sophisticated abroad and we couldn't keep up with them down there. We couldn't afford it and we didn't have the room.

– Ted Hopkins

I think Ted must have been watching too much television at the time. He decided that he wanted the go-go girls to have luminous clothes. He sprayed luminous paint across their knickers. They all got dreadful rashes from the paint. There were more staff in there when they were on than anyone else.

– Wendy, Belrose

arm (a Ted Hopkins' invention hooked up to a car starter motor) holding a box of chocolates covered with a beach towel. As with the Kicking Mules, a ball thrown at a bullseye triggered the arm which hurled the box of chocolates (with Elvis on the front) back to the thrower.

During the 1960s motor cars and television bit into Luna Park's market, offering the public significant entertainment and recreational alternatives.

For a few years in the 1960s, Ted Hopkins presented go-go girls high on stages inside Coney Island above the Turkey Trot.

In 1965 the Park was 30 years old. Ted Hopkins recalled when a long time friend and the biggest showman in America, Paddy Conklin, said: "'Ted, I'm afraid your Park is old hat' and I had to admit it was. I had no one to carry on from me. I thought the best thing to do was get out of it and go fishing".

In April 1969 the remaining six years of the lease and Park contents were sold for $750,000 to a consortium of businessmen called World Trade Centre Pty Ltd, which included Leon Fink, Nathan Spatt and AETNA Life Insurance Company. For a year Ted Hopkins stayed on as caretaker manager to pass on his accumulated knowledge. With the showmen gone, the

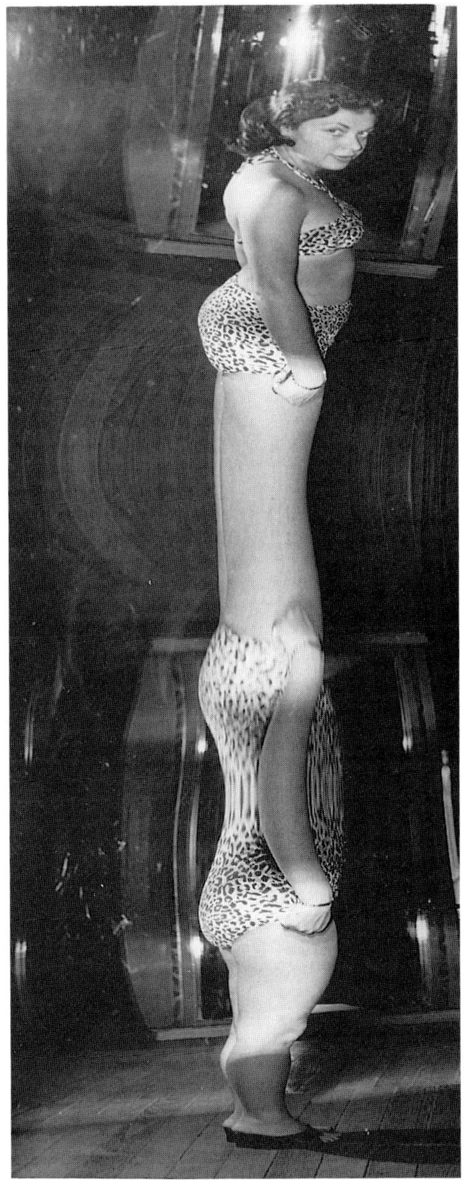

Top: Midway, 1968; *left:* Carousel; *above:* Distorting mirrors.

Top left: Big Dipper; top right: Big Dipper Station; above: Joy Wheel with Turkey Trot in foreground; right: Joy Wheel.

Left: Children on the Spider; *below:* Ted Hopkins (left) and passengers in the Photographic Studio; *bottom:* Big Boy on the Whip, c. 1935.

It was my life. I put everything into it.
– Ted Hopkins

Park's success would depend on the acumen of its new businessmen owners. The full stop had been placed at the end of Luna Park's first sentence.

In 1970, under Ted Hopkins' supervision, the Wild Cat was built by Girvan Bros to replace the Wild Mouse because of its greater capacity. Plans and specifications for the Wild Cat were bought in Germany. Its construction was complex as the size of the ride had to be reduced to fit on the Wild Mouse slab and because Australian steel, being in imperial dimensions, was used for a ride of German metric specifications. Extensive brakes had to be added to pull the cars up.

In the same year Arthur Barton was 81 years old. Ted Hopkins recalled: "It was the most unpleasant thing I had to do. The staff came to see me one day. They said 'Mr Hopkins, if you don't get rid of Arthur Barton, you are going to kill him.' He was driving across the Bridge every day and he was going to kill himself. He was getting too old. I said to him reluctantly, 'Arthur, for your sake, you better retire'." His last work was the Ski Scene on the slides in Coney Island.

Dick Pearce, Eddie Devine and faithful maintenance staff stayed on to ensure the public's safety, but it would take more than their care to protect the public and its prized funfair.

Little did anyone realise that as Ted Hopkins left Luna Park, 21 years of fighting over the land for purposes other than an amusement park was about to begin.

LUNA PARK MILSONS POINT

THE FALL & THE FIGHT

Broadcaster Clive James remarked "In recent years it [Luna Park] had been "...taken over, run down, burned down, abandoned, saved, replanned, abandoned again – the usual dreary process of wondering what to do with vanished glory." It was also speculated upon, fought for, saved again, legislated for, investigated, compensated for, replanned, rebuilt and reopened.

World Trade Centre Pty Ltd applied for a $50 million Harry Seidler-designed International Trade Centre on the Luna Park site – seven high-rise buildings (including a 20 storey building to house all the consulates in Sydney, a 26 storey hotel/motel for 350 visitors, 929,000 square meters of exhibition space and a heliport). Approval was refused because of traffic problems and because the government was determined to preserve what was left of the Sydney Harbour foreshores.

Leon Fink and Nathan Spatt bought out the principal shareholder of World Trade Centre Pty Ltd, AETNA Life Insurance, and formed Luna Park (Holdings) Pty Ltd to continue the site as an amusement park.

Rod Earle, employed as the new general manager, implemented a clean sweep policy eliminating old rides in favour of new thrill rides. Replacement rides had to have a large hourly capacity, allow two people to sit side by side, be ultra safe, be designed and built by a reputable manufacturer, be easily and quickly dismantled and erected elsewhere, and look good by day as well as having complex lighting effects at night. The Flying Saucer and Calypso were removed as they were considered too bland and were not making good returns.

The American entertainment company Hanna-Barbera came up with "The Place where Happiness is" to replace the priceless slogan "Just for Fun". They

Above: Harry Seidler (left) and John Garton (Director, Luna Park Holdings) with World Trade Centre scheme, 1969; *opposite:* Big Dipper.

Above: The Zipper replaces the Tumble Bug ride, 1974; *right:* The Hurricane in the foreground.

also invented Luna Park's answer to Disney's Mickey Mouse – Luna Bear, the space-age Koala.

In December 1971, Urban Systems Corporation prepared a conceptual plan for Lavender Bay that included a waterfront walk, indoor/outdoor theatre, amusement pier, waterfront restaurants and a maritime museum. Clarke Gazzard Architects prepared plans for Luna Park as a part of the scheme.

In 1972 the Park was opened for year-round operation, no longer having a three-month winter closure when rides were thoroughly overhauled and maintained. Time was closing in.

A general program to upgrade the whole Park was started. Maintenance intensive rides such as the Spider and the Tumble Bug were removed. Plans for the Zipper, Hurricane and Astrospin were secured by Rod Earle and built in Australia at a cost of $90,000 each for introduction in December 1973. When these were installed at the front of the Park, the area resembled a parking lot for mobile rides. A lack of bridges accentuated this.

Margaret Fink, then the wife of major shareholder Leon Fink, made the connection between Pop Art and Luna Park. Artists armed with paint and imagination were commissioned to revitalise the Park. Martin Sharp, having completed a colour scheme for the Dodgem Building, repainted the face with the assistance of Tim Lewis, Michael Ramsden and Richard Liney who were also interested in Pop Art. They applied a zigzag motif, topped by geometric clowns' heads and acrylic mirror to the towers. At a cost of $28,000, it was completed in June 1973 to coincide with the opening of the

Left: The Astrospin; *below:* This 1965 Martin Sharp illustration of Minister for Public Works Davis Hughes sparked his interest in Luna Park; *bottom:* HaHa bases on towers of face.

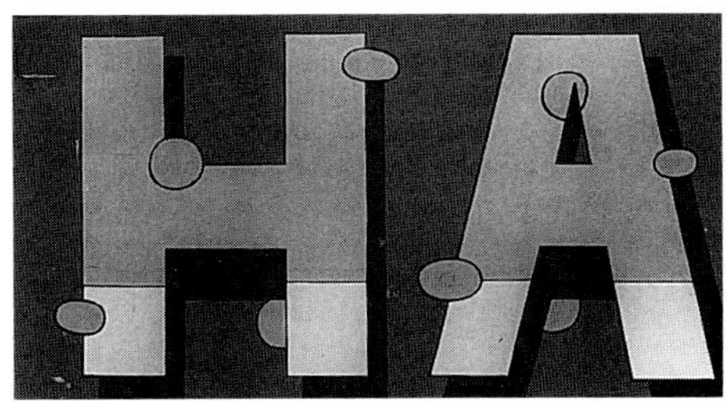

The HAHA was there because Utzon was not asked to the opening and it was looking at the Opera House. It was turned into a big cartoon and made a comment on it.
– Martin Sharp

Sydney Opera House. HaHa was painted on the tower bases. On the back of the face a mandala with a giant psychedelic eye was painted to keep an eye on the Park.

Martin Sharp, Peter Kingston, Richard Liney and Garry Shead also painted the mural, backdrops and signs for Rogues Gallery–Pirate Pete's Sea Battle (the old Bazooka game). Tim Lewis later did colour schemes for Coney Island and the River Caves' mountain. Bruce Petty and Roger Foley were respectively commissioned to prepare schemes for the Ghost Train and River Caves that were never used.

Leigh Hobbs was employed to supervise the repainting of the carousel in September 1974. At first the paint was scratched off the horses. As this was very slow it was decided to dip them in caustic soda. Unfortunately, although a neutralising bath was used and paint was applied over this, the caustic soda penetrated deeply into the wood and later caused rot. Woodcarvers Sel Carr and Harold Wilkinson were employed full-time to remake legs and other parts of the horses. Mirror-backed multifaceted coloured glass jewels from Czechoslovakia were stuck on the horses after Leigh Hobbs painted them.

Right: Back of Martin Sharp face; *opposite:* Martin Sharp face, 1973.

Hoppy never liked the face that I did.
– Martin Sharp

Perhaps they thought artists were just people you hired to do a job. We really put our hearts and souls into the place.
– Martin Sharp

LUNA PAR
Mr Whippy

Above: Proposal for Lavender Bay with Nathan Spatt (left) and Rod Earle, 1975; *below:* Scene in the Photographic Studio, 1970; *opposite:* Martin Sharp (left) and Peter Kingston in the Photographic Studio.

One third of the carousel fretwork was remade, and a new floor and surrounding picket fence were built. Artist Garry Shead painted the wide fascia around the carousel with postcard scenes. The total cost of the carousel renovation was $100,000. Paul Armstrong volunteered his time to restore its 1915 German Gebruder organ. The front of the organ had elaborate Victorian baroque decoration with music motifs and lyre cresting; two front panels of kookaburras had been added by Arthur Barton.

Between April 1975 and April 1976 Leigh Hobbs stripped back to chicken wire the Big Boys and rebuilt them as Larry Luna and Lizzie Luna (now owned by the Powerhouse Museum).

Richard Liney began to restore the Palais in January 1976, painting the interior, remodelling the bar and adding a large mirror decorated with Suzie Wong against a Sydney Harbour background. Later he redesigned the stage. Richard Liney also added the painted fences and lamp posts to the harbour boundary based on the original design. He designed the Crazy Crooners (or Singing Fools game) which was a laughing clown game with heads copied from small porcelain ashtrays where smoke from an ashed cigarette came out the figure's ears. The moulds for the heads were made by artist Arthur Murch.

Richard Liney's final work was the renovation of the Rotor. Not allowed to restore the original facade, he turned to "old science fiction serials, Batman-cum-Metropolis". Consequently a metal-flake finish was applied to the fibro sheets to give the Rotor the appearance of a machine. At the time it was the "largest metal-flaked structure in the Southern Hemisphere". He added a new Rotor sign, a globe to top the facade and the words WHAM WHAM.

This group of artists, who understood and appreciated the work of their artistic predecessors, were the founding members of Friends of Luna Park.

In July 1974 six teeth were stolen from the face.

In July 1975 another scheme designed by Urban Systems Corporation was revealed which would turn the Lavender Bay foreshores into a Tivoli Gardens type area that included Luna Park. At the same time a $2 entry fee was introduced which would entitle patrons to 14 rides. Prior to this rides had been 35¢ for children and 70¢ for adults, with free admission.

Nathan Spatt's son, Maurice, was appointed general manager in September 1975. His priority was "to replace chicken wire with creepers and natural wood". Illusion began to revert to reality. Ted Hopkins had kept landscaping out of his Park because he said it settled people down – the last thing he wanted in an amusement park.

The lease expired in October 1975. Operations continued on a weekly basis. New lease documents were being drawn up and given preliminary approval by the Liberal Government. Plans for a restaurant designed by Harry Seidler in "the shape of an ice cream cone" on top of the cliff were revealed. In May 1976, Neville Wran's Labor Party ousted the Liberal Government and lease negotiations virtually ceased. The *Australian Financial Review* (22 March 1981) reported that "Luna Park Pty Ltd's

LUNA
PARK

Right: Ghost Train, 1973; *opposite top and bottom:* Ghost Train fire, 1979.

All the boys went to holy communion before they died, so we know they went straight to heaven.

– Jason Holman

It was their first time there and they probably thought that the smoke from the fire was part of the ride.

– Mr Rahilly

spokesman believes the company lost favour with the State Labor Government after allegedly criticising in a restaurant a trip the Premier took on a prominent businessman's plane during a plane strike."

> Had Wran not interfered with the process, the Park would never have closed, it would have been fully upgraded, retained all its original charm and have been accessible for many years and not be costing the government whatever the all-up figure is now to put it back again. – Leon Fink

The Zumur arrived from America in October 1976 to replace the Spider. During 1977 and 1978 palms were planted along the Midway.

The Friends of Luna Park held an exhibition called "Fairground Arts and Novelties" at the end of 1977 at the Art Gallery of New South Wales to exhibit the remnants that had made Luna Park so special.

Cinema 180 opened on the Tumble Bug site in May 1979. Movies were projected onto the ceiling showing stampedes, falling through the Grand Canyon, rushing down Niagara Falls and screaming down on a roller coaster. The external murals were painted by Peter Kingston and Garry Shead.

On 16 April 1979, 13 people were injured on the Big Dipper when a steel runner came loose and halted a Dipper carriage. The following carriage rammed into its rear, injuring the occupants. A warning had been served.

On Cracker Night, 9 June 1979, no Sydney trains were running due to a rail strike. The Big Dipper was still being repaired. The Ghost Train was the only train operating in Sydney that night. A minimum of three attendants were usually needed to operate the Ghost Train – an operator, a ticket collector and a third person who patrolled the interior for any mischief. On

this night, there were only two staff, leaving the interior unpatrolled and vulnerable. What was not supposed to happen happened. A fire broke out and quickly spread in the timber building with its bitumen-covered roof. There were no sprinklers and water pressure was low.

The charred rubble revealed the bodies of six children and one adult. John Godson, returning from holidays with his sons Damien and Craig, decided to visit Luna Park and Taronga Zoo on their way home. Waverley College students Jonathan Billings, Richard Carroll, Michael Johnson and Seamus Rahilly had been to Mass on their way to Luna Park.

Luna Park was closed from that night. Luna Park's second sentence was complete.

Dr A.D. Stokes, a senior lecturer of electrical engineering, testified at the coronial inquiry that the fire did not start through failure of permanent wiring within the ride. Witnesses claimed seeing a mock fire scene which consisted of red streamers blown by a fan to simulate real fire.

Coroner Kevin Anderson criticised the Park's owners for what he termed their reluctance to implement safety measures. As early as mid-1977, North Sydney Council had given Luna Park 18 months to fulfil Board of Fire Commissioners' requirements. At the time of the fire these had all

Right: Stripped carousel horse head;
below: Restored carousel horse;
bottom: Restored lion on carousel.

been carried out except for the emergency lighting and hose reel system. The Coroner concluded that it was most unlikely that ignition occurred through an electrical fault, that the two fire hoses outside (one of which did not have a nozzle on it) were not long enough to deal effectively with the fire, and that the smell of smoke was ignored for five minutes. The Coroner's report went on:

> The company, Luna Park Pty Ltd, its directors and management were under a duty of care in respect of the safety of its patrons. The fire was reasonably foreseeable. The death to, or injury to patrons by fire was reasonably foreseeable. There was a failure in duty of care. Although there was a serious breach of the duty of care, there was not, in my view, that high degree of negligence necessary to support a charge involving criminal negligence.

Three weeks later one of the spires on the entry towers collapsed while being repaired. The other spire was removed for symmetry. Luna Park was thoroughly exhausted.

Tenders were called on 31 July 1979 for the use of the site. This was subsequently withdrawn as tenderers complained that the application period was too short and that the one-and-a-half page tender document was too loosely worded. Responsibility shifted from the Department of Lands and Services to the Premier's Department with Deputy Premier Jack Ferguson chairing the selection committee.

Above: Letterhead by Martin Sharp; *below:* Letterhead by Peter Kingston.

Realising the gravity of the situation, the artists who made up Friends of Luna Park were joined by people of all backgrounds, professions, ages and municipalities to preserve Luna Park. They staged a second Luna Park exhibition in September 1979 at the National Trust Centre. Soon after a third exhibition was held at OTC House in Martin Place.

A second round of tenders was called in August for submission on 31 August 1979; the date was extended first to 26 October and then to 23 November 1979. Luna Park (Holdings) Ltd and Camingo Pty Ltd (a Reg Grundy Organisation company) had similar tenders which proposed keeping and upgrading the existing Park. New sections to the Camingo proposal had a futuristic theme designed by architect John Andrews.

As early as 1976 architects Thiessen & Associates had proposed a $50 million development on land that included Luna Park. Their proposal contained a multistorey hotel, marina, car park and Snugglepot and Cuddlepie theme park. Only a copy of the face was to be retained on the side of a Ferris wheel. Previous general manager Rod Earle was commissioned as their consultant. Thiessen & Associates designed the proposal,

Jokingly at first, we talked about what fun it would be to re-open Luna Park for our grandchildren, of which we both have several. Then, somehow, we stopped joking and became serious. Why not, we asked ourselves.

– *Col Goldstein*

CALLING ALL KIDS & EVERYONE

SAVE LUNA PARK

ON SATURDAY 28TH JUNE 1980

☆ **WALK FROM OPERA HOUSE TO LUNA PARK** MEET AT THE OPERA HOUSE AT. 12. NOON.

☆ **PARTY AT LUNA PARK 2.PM TO 5.PM**

☆ **MENTAL AS ANYTHING** + BUNDEENA KIDS PLAY "LUNA PARKS LONG LASTING LAUGH" ☆ LETS COMPLETELY RESTORE LUNA PARK WITH ITS ARCHITECTURE AND CHARACTER, ITS PRESENT NAME AND BELOVED DISTINCTIVE SITE BUT VERY VERY SAFE! ☆☆ JUST FOR FUN ☆☆

☆ FOR FURTHER INFORMATION RING "THE FRIENDS OF LUNA PARK".

KINGO 9226191, SAM 3576787, DAVID 901481, ALISTER 365387, MARTIN 365745

Opposite: Handbill by Friends of Luna Park, 1980; *left:* Handbill by Friends of Luna Park, 1980.

We consider Luna Park an item of national interest.
– North Sydney Alderman Sybil Kesteven

People may be apathetic about whether it's pulled down now but if they hear those bull-dozers, the whole nation will rise up.
– Brett Whiteley

A Disneyland can be built anywhere but Luna Park as we know it is irreplaceable as a part of Sydney's history.
– Carol Baker, Mayor North Sydney Council

Smiles are rare in a big city and are worth holding on to.
– Kenneth Kennedy, Paddington, Letters to the Editor Sydney Morning Herald, *26 October 1979*

Luna Park should be demolished and the site turned into a public park.
– Peter Manson, Darlinghurst Letters to the Editor, Sydney Morning Herald, *12 February 1980*

I just want to go past that big face again.
– Bette Midler

I am very concerned about what happens to various parts of Sydney, but secondly, I am particularly concerned in this case because I happen to occupy an office which overlooks Luna Park and over the years I have grown to love it dearly.
–Harry Seidler

then found a client, Australian Leisure Enterprises – a consortium of National Mutual Insurance, Ampol Petroleum and the Southern Pacific Hotel Corporation (Travelodge). Alpat and Bullens of Bullens Circus were also reported as tendering.

On 17 January 1980 all tenders were rejected. The government claimed that none met the requirement to provide amenities similar to those available before the Park was closed and none had guaranteed continuous lease payments to the government for 30 years.

A third round of tenders was called on 12 March 1980 for submission

Face in disrepair, 1981.

Certainly much should be preserved such as the twenties artwork of Arthur Barton, the magnificent merry-go-round and the modern rides since 1971. Most of the rest should be torn down and a new start should be made.

– Rod Earle

I don't call that art.
– Gisella Scheinberg, Holdsworth Galleries

on 17 June 1980. Keeping their options open, Luna Park (Holdings) Pty Ltd applied to Holroyd Council to move their rides to a disused brickpit at Merrylands.

The final six tenders were Luna Park (Holdings) Ltd, Camingo, Far East Hotels and Entertainments Ltd, A.W. Edwards (a Balmain construction firm), Australian Amusements Associates and Opinion Project Analysis Pty Ltd (Thiessen & Associates' retender of the Australian Leisure Enterprises' second tender without the highrise hotel).

The Tender Assessment Committee was chaired by Jack Halliday, the Undersecretary of the Department of Services, and consisted of the Undersecretary of the Department of Lands, the Valuer-General, Andrew Andersons as a representative of the Government Architect, and representatives of the Planning and Environment Commission and the Premier's Department.

While the tenders were being considered, Friends of Luna Park staged a "Save Luna Park Day" on 28 June 1980. Support for the traditional Luna Park was demonstrated by a protest march from the Opera House over the Bridge to the Face where a free concert appropriately headlined by rock group Mental as Anything included a play by Bundeena school children – "Luna's Longest Lasting Laugh". Friends of Luna Park was concerned that one of the world's last traditional amusement parks would become a casino or an American style theme park. At the rally, it was announced that, at the Friends request, the National Trust had classified the face and towers as items of national heritage, and given the rest of the Park a "recorded" classification.

On 13 July 1980 Friends of Luna Park held a public meeting in the Lower Sydney Town Hall. Speakers supporting Luna Park included Harry Seidler, Jack Mundy, Leo Schofield, John Morris and Professor Peter Johnson. On 17 October 1980 Friends of Luna Park were commissioned by the Department of Public Works to prepare a report on the significance of Luna Park.

A lease was granted on 23 September 1980 to Australian Amusements Associates (who were later known as Harbourside Amusements Pty Ltd). The *Australian* headline read "Edgley Wins the Battle for Luna Park".

Harbourside Amusements consisted of Sir Arthur George (solicitor, businessman and president of the Australia Soccer Federation), brothers Harold and Colman Goldstein (the latter an engineer in the kitchen and refrigeration business), Michael Edgley (entrepreneur) and Brian Treasure. Edgley officially resigned a year later. He was replaced on the board by David Baffsky of the legal firm Simons & Baffsky.

The government granted the tender to Harbourside Amusements because they promised low-cost family entertainment and guaranteed a minimum annual rent of $250,000. The promise of retaining certain historic buildings was expected to appease Friends of Luna Park. Edgley's participation gave the proposal an entertainment flavour. In return for the 30 year lease, Harbourside promised to build Kiddieland, an open air water slide,

Above: Face in 1980; *left:* Richard Liney (left), Peter Kingston and Martin Sharp dressed as Redcoats.

I'll miss the place. It's part of the childhood of almost everyone in Sydney.
– Dick Pearce on being retrenched with the rest of the staff on 11 February 1980

It took us a while to realise that Luna Park was an artwork in itself, a city state of illusion, a brilliant feat of engineering with imagination, created and maintained by a unique band of men. Sydney must acknowledge the importance of Luna Park. To lose it now would be a tragedy.
– Martin Sharp

Left: Lizzie Luna and Larry Luna; *below:* Dodgem cars.

Left: The Rotor; *bottom left:* Popeye outside Coney Island, 1979; *below:* Coney Island.

I'm not interested in a tired old park.... We will not buy the crummy old equipment that is there.

– Col Goldstein

dodgems, video and pinball machines, a Superloop, a Pirate Ship and a child-care centre. An entry fee of $2.50 was to include ten rides.

Valuations were sought following a dispute between Luna Park (Holdings) and Harbourside over the value of some of the fittings on the site. Luna Park (Holdings) acquired valuations from Hogarth Galleries of $196,000 and Macquarie Galleries of $111,200. Harbourside's valuations were from Australian Art Auctions of $2,020; and Holdsworth Galleries which said "They have no value". A sum of $500,000 was finally agreed on for all the fittings.

On 13 April 1981 the Luna Park Site Bill was passed which forced Luna Park (Holdings) to vacate the site 27 days earlier than specified by the lease. After 3 June 1981 a fine of $1,000.00 per day would be imposed. This bill was passed to avoid further legal battles over the lease with Luna Park (Holdings).

In November 1980 Harry Seidler was again offered the commission to design a restaurant on top of the cliff now adjacent to his offices.

Leon Fink and Nathan Spatt sold several transportable rides to Hollywood Pleasure Grounds at Lansvale, "the Luna Park of the West".

On a rainy 31 May and 1 June 1981, an auction was held within Luna Park to sell anything detachable. Larry Freels, a collector from San Francisco, paid $140,000 for the carousel and $20,000 for the Gebruder organ. The carousel animals were shipped back to America. The shipping agent tried to sell the mechanical mechanism locally and finally kept it in lieu of a fee for disassembly and crating.

Friends of Luna Park bought the Barrels of Fun, Turkey Trot and Joy Wheel for $9,200 to keep them in the Park. They also bought the River Caves for $20.

In these two days, Luna Park, including the name, was dismembered and scattered about Sydney.

On 3 June 1981 Col Goldstein entered the site and began demolition. The Wild Cat and Carousel were dismantled and removed. The Big Dipper, Davy Jones Locker and River Caves were bulldozed and burnt.

Above: Mick Carpenter (left), Richard Liney, Peter Kingston and Martin Sharp; *opposite top:* Peter Kingston and Pirate Pete's Sea Battle; *opposite bottom:* Mask from "Luna Park's Long Lasting Laugh" by school children from Bundeena, 1980.

People went nostalgia mad and bought almost anything...I guess the park meant a lot to many people and they were buying memories.

– Gary, auctioneer

Above: Central skeleton on Ghost Train;
right: Crazy Crooner game.

Left: River Caves mountain; *bottom left and below:* Mermaids from King Neptune scene in the River Caves.

Above: Water Skooters; *right:* Arthur Barton mural in Coney Island; *opposite:* Fireworks over Luna Park.

Above: Defaced with fibreglass mould; *right:* Fibreglass face, 1982.

The River Caves does not fit into the new park.

– *Col Goldstein*

The cheapest amusement park in the country.

– *Col Goldstein*

I always thought it was a very comforting sight to the see that great grinning face as you came across the Harbour.

– *Frank Crooke, ABC Radio 2BL*

Ten million dollars bought a second-hand roller coaster called the Geronimo (underneath which were dodgems, games and a shooting gallery), an Australian made 35 metre Ferris wheel called Skylab, a Superloop, a Pirate Ship and a Wave Swinger. Most rides were imported. The Rotor and Cinema 180, although given facelifts, remained much as they had been. Unbuilt promises included a water chute, a BMX track, a roller-skating rink, a waterfall into a lake, a ride where children could propel themselves with a joy stick to shoot their opponents out of the sky and a big dipper that Col Goldstein claimed "was the best money could buy".

The designers were LARC International of Dallas, Texas. Their distinctive American flavour was reflected in the transformation of the Palais de Danse into a Mississippi steamer, the Harbour Queen, with a restaurant inside. Fairy Floss was blue. The entry fee nearly doubled to $4.50 ($5.50 on Sundays).

A cast was taken from the face so a replica could be made. Surfboard

Left: Harbour Queen, 1988;
above: Harbourside Amusement Park, 1982.

makers Darryl Holmes and Stephen Johnson grappled with difficult task of working with facial features on such a huge scale. They repaired the face then made a fibreglass mould and demolished the original face. The mould was reinforced and reinstated but it was a poor copy of Martin Sharp's clown face with a lumpy forehead, bloodshot eyeballs and pupils that were in the centre of the eye opening – the position of the eye when terrified.

The reconstructed face said a lot about the Park behind. Obscuring the Park's priceless advertisement of itself, ticket booths were constructed in front of the mouth.

The Park opened as Harbourside Amusement Park on 29 April 1982. A dispute with the previous owners prevented the use of the name Luna Park until August.

The Department of Public Works commissioned a study of the face that recommended it be rebuilt complete with spires to mark the Park's approaching fiftieth birthday. Harbourside Amusements ignored the recommendation.

Plans for a massive Arrow Huss roller coaster running the full length of the Park were revealed in August 1984. The only catch was that to fit it on the site, Coney Island would have to be demolished. Harbourside approached the Museum of Applied Arts and Sciences to determine whether they would take the building. A report commissioned by the Department of Public Works on the importance of Coney Island recommended its retention. The dominoes were beginning to fall.

Independent member of Parliament John Hatton raised questions in Parliament "of any relationship between one or more of the directors [of Harbourside] and Mr Abraham Saffron" in October 1985. Six months later the Attorney General announced that an investigation to answer these questions would take place. The Corporate Affairs Commission report revealed that Arcadia Amusements and Vending Pty Ltd (which hired arcade machines to Harbourside Amusements) was controlled by Abe Saffron who

We now have a McDonald's image.
– Harold Droga
Managing Director, Harbourside

Right: Paul Zanetti cartoon of Neville Wran; *below:* Martin Sharp ink drawing; *bottom:* Warren Brown cartoon, 1988.

The fire couldn't have been attempted unless the perpetrators were completely confident that they could get away with it. Their confidence was misplaced. The fear generated by the deaths was designed to silence any questions about the possibility that the fire was anything but an unfortunate act. It didn't.

– Martin Sharp

It must not become another Darling Harbour, or a place used primarily by the occupants of hotels or offices.

– Ros Crichton

was related to Col and Harold Goldstein. Harbourside's company secretary and onetime financial controller, Samuel Cowper, was Abe Saffron's nephew and was also a director of Marshin Holdings Pty Ltd whose other directors were Abe Saffron's mother and sister. Cowper was later replaced by Roy Travers from Simons & Baffsky. David Baffsky had had "extensive professional dealings" with Abe Saffron. Another Harbourside director, Brian Treasure "also revealed that he had a business relationship with Mr Saffron". Nevertheless the report concluded that "there was no evidence available to the delegates that suggests that Abraham Gilbert Saffron has any actual or beneficial ownership in Harbourside."

Two years later the National Crime Authority reopened investigations into the Ghost Train fire.

Prome Investments Pty Ltd were quietly negotiating with the government to transfer the lease and extend it to 99 years. At this time Harbourside directors were Col and Harold Goldstein, Harold Droga and David Baffsky. Prome was a consortium consisting of Dr Alistair Stone (managing director), Citistate Corporation Limited, the Carringbush Corporation limited, Genoa Resources and Investments Limited, Entrad Corporation Limited and Tricontinental Corporation Limited. Plans revealed restaurants, nightclubs, cinemas and cafes.

Luna Park was allowed to close on 10 April 1988 for "renovations and repairs" as recommended by an engineer's report. Prome changed its name to Luna Park Investments Pty Ltd in May. David Baffsky, also a director of Club Mediterranee (Aust) Pty Ltd met with Nick Greiner in July to discuss the possibilities of a resort on the site. The lease was transferred to Luna

Above: Senior and junior citizens at Friends of Luna Park rally, August 1989; *left:* Ros Crichton addressing supporters at the Friends of Luna Park rally, August 1989.

It really is the end of an era. Now it will be a tourist centre rather than a people's place.
– Ted Mack, Independent Federal Member of Parliament for North Sydney

Hands off our childhoods.
– protest banner

Luna Park, if it had been conserved, would have been a showpiece.
– Bob Carr, NSW Labor Party leader

The trouble with the Luna Park site is that it has always been driven by greed.
–Robyn Read

The Government's plan looks like a Nazi holiday camp.
– Robyn Read

The face is a symbol of the gateway to fantasy and I don't think we are going to let them get away with this one.
– Genia McCaffrey

Luna Park is to enjoy not to destroy.
– Marcia, Cremorne

A funfair is not appropriate for the 1990s.
– Rob Dempsey
Promenade general manager

People power has finally won. The saving of Luna Park shows idealism lives in a city that has been for so long dominated by greed.
– Robyn Read

Park Investments in November. On 30 November 1988 the towers were demolished as a Heritage Council order preventing the demolition of the towers and face was allowed to lapse. The face was relocated on the Park site. The towers were chainsawed down and dumped.

In December the Deputy Premier and Minister for State Development Wal Murray announced that plans for highrise development on the site had been refused and that any development would have to retain the original character of the amusement park.

North Sydney Council, under Mayors Ted Mack and Ros Crichton supported by Alderman Robyn Read, was consistently diligent to prevent unsympathetic development on the Luna Park site. In February 1989 the Director of the Department of Planning revoked North Sydney Council's powers to certify a new Local Environmental Plan for Luna Park and the adjacent railway land which would prevent previously allowed tourist facilities. North Sydney Council then prepared a Development Control Plan for the site, restricting development to two stories above the cliff and three below. Advice for this plan was received from Andrew Andersons, Peter Webber, Martin Sharp and Peter Kingston.

State government guidelines allowed buildings to a height of nine metres adjacent to the harbour, equal to the top of the cliff adjacent to the cliff and to 21 metres on top of the cliff. The guidelines allowed "tourist and recreation facilities" which included hotels, motels and marinas. Luna Park's face and towers, Ferris wheel, Coney Island, the Palais and the Dodgem Building were "suggested" for retention.

A scheme leaked to the *Sydney Morning Herald* revealed the full extent of the Luna Park Investments' development – a 200 room hotel, 1,200 space car park and an office block over Coney Island.

Friends of Luna Park gained the backing of a fresh group of supporters from all over Sydney at a public meeting organised at North Sydney Council on 30 March 1989. To highlight a forthcoming rally at Luna Park and to mark the tenth anniversary of the Ghost Train fire, Friends of Luna Park erected banners from the Ridge Street footbridge in North Sydney attracting the attention of morning commuters heading on to the Harbour Bridge.

Two thousand people attended the protest rally in front of where the face once was on 27 August 1989. Colourful radio personality Maynard F# Crabbes compered the day of performances donated by the Castanet Club, Ignatius Jones, Café at the Gates of Salvation, Terry Serio, Gary Shearston and the Hummingbirds.

Attack was coming from all fronts. Both Robyn Read and Harry Seidler applied unsuccessfully for Freedom of Information requests into the lease negotiations. In November 1989 Friends of Luna Park met with Premier Nick Greiner who now had Luna Park in his personal control.

Promenade Investments, the new name for Luna Park Investments, were given nine months to fulfil their current lease obligations and to open Luna Park as an amusement park by 1 June 1990.

On 16 May Promenade held a press conference to put on public record

what they proposed for the site. In the last weeks before 1 June, rides were moved around the site to give the appearance that Promenade were trying as hard as they could. Squirming for excuses, with only 48 hours to go, they did the impossible – self imposed a union ban on the site, claiming asbestos in the old buildings. The presence of the same asbestos cement sheet had not prevented their demolition of the face and towers. When the ultimatum expired, Friends of Luna Park wearing the traditional masks from the Park were outside armed with placards:

COME OUT WITH YOUR HANDS UP – SYDNEY HAS YOU CORNERED.

LUNA PARK – UNJUST FOR FUN

The lease was terminated on 5 June 1990 through the Luna Park Site Act 1990. "The Bill provides for the Luna Park Site to be vested in the Crown and dedicated for public recreation, public amusement and public entertainment" (Wal Murray).

Days later the National Trust classified the site as well as the individual items on it. The Luna Park Site Act was gazetted on 12 October 1990:

> The object of the Bill is to return the Luna Park Site to the people of New South Wales and to ensure that Luna Park and the associated harbour foreshore remain available and accessible for the enjoyment of the people of New South Wales.

The Bill established a Trust to produce a plan of management to determine an appropriate use for the site.

The inaugural Luna Park Reserve Trust was a diverse range of people

Opposite & above: Friends of Luna Park protest, 1 June 1990; *below:* Promenade scheme for Lavender Bay, May 1990.

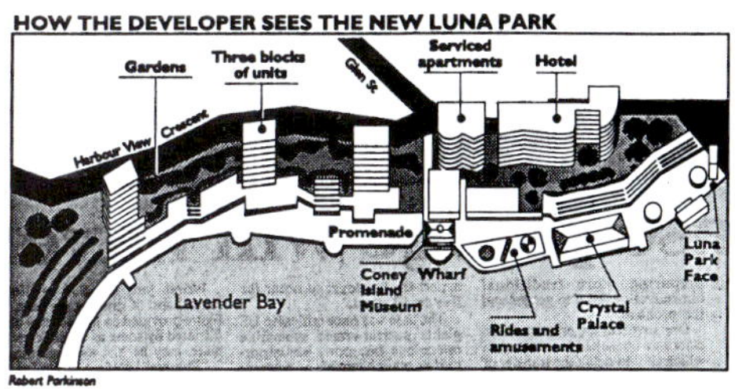

Above: ABC newsreader Richard Morecroft; *right:* Cartoon by Jenny Coopes, June 1990.

The raising of the asbestos and sea wall issues at this late date is nothing more than a pretext to cover Promenade's own failure to comply with the notice, indicating that the lessees have never been serious about restoring Luna Park.

– Wal Murray

Above: Channel 9 newsreader Brian Henderson; *far left:* Australia Post postmark for North Sydney Post Office; *left: Daily Mirror* billboard, June 1990.

If Mr Greiner doesn't restore Luna Park's laughing face, he will go down in history as leader of the government that wiped the smile off the face of Sydney forever.
– Barbara, North Sydney

Above: Matthew Martin cartoon, June 1990; *right:* Model of Wittingslow proposal.

It took me three months to build it but three years for you people to think about what to do with it.

– Ted Hopkins to Nick Greiner

I've made it clear that I think Luna Park is the single most important project that could get attention.

– Nick Greiner

with a wide range of skills. Chairman John Armstrong was a local resident as well as merchant banker. Graham Nock had been president of the Bicentennial Decorations Committee and a company director. Andrew Andersons as head of Public Work's Special Projects had expertise on specialised government projects and had commissioned several definitive reports on Luna Park. Leo Schofield had voiced support for Luna Park and had extensive experience in public relations. He had already been commissioned to determine the make-up of the Trust. Both Robyn Read and Roslyn Crichton had town planning as well as local and state government skills, in particular public representation and accountability. Sam Marshall had written the history of Luna Park as well as been a Friend of Luna Park since 1979. Derek Sinclair from the Department of Conservation and Land Management was appointed executive secretary.

Leo Schofield was replaced in 1994 by Anne Fulwood who brought her media skills to the Trust. Genia McCaffery, a spokesperson for Friends of Luna Park since 1989, replaced Ros Crichton as a person active in the North Sydney community.

Arbitration hearings before Sir Laurence Street which began on 18 October 1990 concluded that Promenade be paid $3,500,000 compensation for the value of the lease ($23 million had been claimed).

Nine months later a plan of management was submitted by project managers McLachlan Consultants and architect Bruce Eeles. The first two stages were approved in 1991 and $25 million from the Open Space and Heritage

Below: Sydney Morning Herald cartoon by Jeremy; *bottom:* Elevation of proposed Luna Park, 1994.

...so we actively bring Luna Park to life again because that's what I expect the overwhelming majority of New South Wales would want.

–Nick Greiner

Above: Photomontage of proposed Luna Park, 1994; *right:* Face being moved to the Powerhouse Museum, 1994.

I lived all my life in Cliff Street until 7 years ago. The noise from Luna Park was – wonderful. It was the noise of people having a wonderful time.

– Nancy, Artarmon

I'd like to see green grass with sheep grazing on Luna Park.

– Resident at public meeting 28.11.92

Luna Park is Australia's greatest example of the great Australian ugliness. We celebrated when it closed down.

– Carol, Lavender Bay

Fund was given to upgrade the site and to place a boardwalk around Luna Park and adjacent railway land. For the first time people would be able to walk from Watt Park around Lavender Bay past or through Luna Park, to Kirribilli, enjoying magnificent views of Sydney along the way. The third stage (not approved) would be to remove the railway storage and spur line for parkland, an amphitheatre, gallery and museum. Overcome by the spell of Luna Park, then Minister for Conservation and Land Management Garry West thanked the "Historic Trousers Trust" (instead of the Historic Houses Trust) for holding the function when funding was announced.

Ken Maher and Partners in association with Paul Berkemeier were appointed architects. On 17 August 1992, a week before the Luna Park plans were approved by North Sydney Council, Ted Hopkins died aged 90. He had previously been shown the plans for the new Luna Park that was to be built where he had first built Luna Park 57 years before. He was pleased with what he saw. The commencement of construction of the Trust works by Concrete Constructions was marked by Garry West as the face was moved back to its former location on 20 January 1993.

To provide quality and avoid the previous problems with leases, the Trust determined to lease the various functions to experts in their respective fields. The Wittingslow Amusements Group, headed in Sydney by third-generation showman Des Wittingslow Jnr, became the preferred amusements operator.

Wittingslow sought equity investors to add to their own contribution in order to bring about their vision. As an agreement could not be reached, the equity proposal was rejected by the Trust. Instead Luna Park Amusements Pty Ltd was established to develop and operate the Park with both the Trust and Wittingslow contibuting. To borrow funds collectively, Wittingslow contributed their rides and cash and the Trust contributed some of its assets on the site. As a consequence Wittingslow's architects, McConnell Smith & Johnson, joined the team of architects.

As a re-run of when Luna Park was first proposed in Lavender Bay, some residents vocally opposed the restitution of Luna Park. Traditionally Luna Park fitted well into the community with most residents overlooking the noise of people having fun across the bay. Since 1935 the Luna Park site has only been zoned for amusements. People moving into the area during the time Luna Park was closed purchased with full knowledge that Luna Park would one day reopen.

Two Freedom of Information applications were served on the Trust from a firm of solicitors who refused to name their client. When the managing director of rival fun park Australia's Wonderland was asked by the *Sydney Morning Herald* whether they were involved in the first application, he replied "Yes, we have been involved".

On 22 May 1994 George Souris, Minister for Conservation and Land Management, donated the face to Minister for the Arts, Peter Collins, to be located at the Powerhouse Museum. Luna Park had been accepted into the popular culture hall of fame.

Luna Park Reserve Trust logo, 1994.

When it comes to Luna Park, there is no last straw.

– Chris Mangin
General Manager, Luna Park Reserve Trust

Luna Park is being returned to the city. It's ours. It belongs to us.

– John Armstrong

Luna Park face awaits the verdict, 1980.

LUNA PARK MILSONS POINT

FANTASY & THE FUTURE

The history of Luna Park is a window to the strange behaviour of human beings. Ted Hopkins epitomised this with his saying "You know, the public are funny people".

Luna Park, as the land that reality forgot, had something for everyone. It was an asylum for refugees from everyday life. It was a safety valve to the pressure of life. It was a social tonic and a laboratory of emotions and experiences. It was the biggest dating service, biggest toy box and biggest child-minding service in Australia. It was the land where the silly season lasted all year. It was the land where something awful was always about to happen. It was a land where only Luna Parkese was spoken. It was the land of deception where one was made a fool of if it was for the amusement of all. It was the world in microcosm. It was Sydney humour on the harbour. It was a mirror capable of reversing the norm. For the artistic, it was a lode with an abundance of gems waiting to be mined. The multiplicity and unashamed dishonesty of its images gave the Park its unity. Anything went, as all was for fun.

Luna Park on Coney Island brought together many disparate ingredients to create a truly unique phenomenon. The combination included the carnival, the theatre, the zoo, physics, psychology, the very latest technology, the aspirations of a rapidly-changing industrialised population and the immortal desire to be amused. This infectious formula spread right across America and around the world. Luna Parks were established in most major cities such as Paris, Berlin, Tel Aviv and Tokyo.

Created 11 years after Luna Park Coney Island, Luna Park St Kilda was able to draw on the successes and failures of not only these Luna Parks but also other great amusement centres such as Blackpool. The best ideas were openly

Right: Ted Hopkins in front of his caricature with spanner in the Coney Island mural of the building of Luna Park by Arthur Barton; *opposite:* Shields from Penny Arcade painted by Arthur Barton including caricatures of Ted Hopkins *(left in top centre)*, David Atkins *(right in top centre)*, Dick Pearce *(top right)*, Norm Portman *(bottom left)*, and Ted Hopkins *(right in bottom centre)*.

SEE WHAT YOUR FUTURE HUSBAND WILL BE LIKE
PUT PENNY IN SLOT→
BLIND

WHEN SEARCHING AROUND THE PARK'S FULL LENGTH, IF YOU FIND THESE TWO, YOU'VE FOUND THE STRENGTH !!

THE INQUISITIVE THIN MAN
WORKSHOP

GIRLS !!
CHOOSE THE STRONG ATHLETIC TYPE !!

THE SHORTSIGHTED CUSTOMER
PENNIES HERE

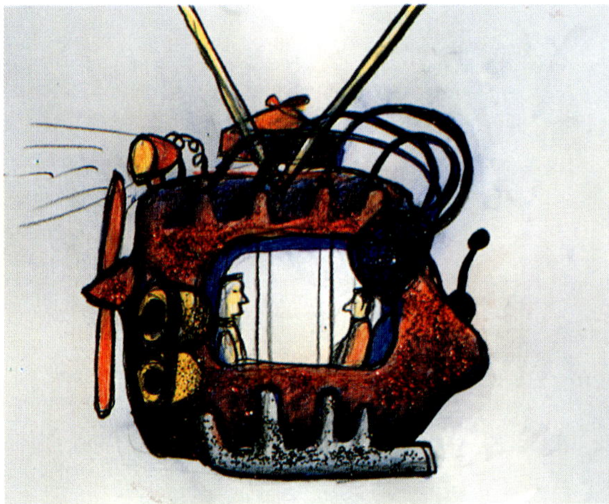

borrowed. Tried and tested attractions and methods were in turn tested on the Australian public. The results were verified in Glenelg which proved a success despite a small population, an economic depression and an unsympathetic local community. The alternative site in Sydney was well worth the move and the subsequent battles: it was one of the best locations in the world for an amusement park – on a beautiful harbour right in the centre of the city.

By the 1920s most Luna Parks in America had disappeared. In Australia the evolution continued. In 1995 the lost world of Luna Park was not simply being recreated – its evolution is continuing. Rebuilding the old Luna Park would be an anathema to its very manifesto.

Luna Park is an eclectic mix, appearing as if it had never become run down and closed. To maintain its patronage, Luna Park always developed and changed, even if the rides were only repainted and moved about the Park. The best attractions from the past have been returned and the very latest introduced. Nostalgia is a touchstone for those with memories to brag about to their children. New attractions keep pace with novelty. Like the city, Luna Park will never stop evolving.

Those who would have lost the most had Luna Park not returned – the children – were the least able to stage a campaign of public agitation. The Friends of Luna Park fought their long struggle against seemingly hopeless odds.

Much is revealed about the nature of Sydney by the fact that an amusement park can be established, thrive and be revived although located on such an important and valuable site between two major business centres in Australia. Luna Park has the honour of being the only amusement park (perhaps apart from Tivoli Gardens in Copenhagen) to be protected by legislation and embraced by a whole city.

Weeks, months and years of delirious anticipation are over. Luna Park is again open. This time the people of New South Wales own it and will benefit from its success.

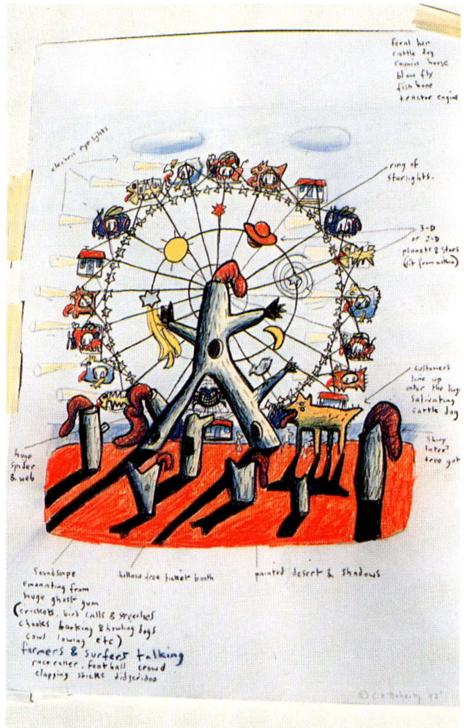

Proposed designs for Ferris Wheel and carriages *(opposite)* by Reg Mombassa, 1993.

REFERENCES

The main written sources for information contained in this book follow. Other sources of information have been the Stanton Library's Local Studies Collection, the Victorian Performing Arts Museum and Martin Sharp's records.

Much of the oral history information came from interviews by the author with the following:

Peter Anderson, 7 June 1993
Cryil Brown, 23 June 1993
Les Christian, 31 January 1994
Hazel Court, 28 May 1993
Don Cox, 19 March 1994
Cecelia Daniels, 2 December 1993
Eddie Devine, 10 November, 3 December 1992
Noelene Dresser, 28 May 1993
Leon Fink, 29 April 1994, 5 May 1994
George French, 4 November 1992
Merle Gamon, 13 December 1993
Bob Gordon, 22 June 1993
Shelley Grey, 13 May 1993
Les & Pat Hart, 4 December 1993
Kim Hilder, 3 February 1994
Peter Hooker, 3 February 1994
Ted Hopkins, 3 July, 17 July, 24 July, 31 July 1990
Harry Howard, 21 March 94
Frank Hughes, many phone conversations
Pat Hutchings, 29 September 1993
Tom Ingram, 2 December 1993
Peter Kingston, 30 March, 13 April 1993
Roy Langford, 3 February 1994
Alice McIntyre, 28 May 1993
Eileen McMillan, 21 September 1993
Tony & Wendy Maloney, 28 July 1992
Nigel Markov, 7 December 1993
Mandy Marshall, 2 December 1993
Ronald Newland, 2 August 1993
Alan Osborne, 11 January 1994
Bruce & John Patience, 4 December 1993
Dick & Blanche Pierce, 27 June, 11 July 1993, 22 March 1994
Eric Platt, 4 December 1993
Ken Potts, 3 February 1994
Les Powell, 5 December 1993
Joyce Rogers, 30 March 1994
S. John Ross, 3 May 1993
Dorothy Salau, 4 December 1993
Bert Saville, 4 December 1993
Keith Searle, 12 August 1994
Martin Sharp, 10 May 1993, 8 March 1994
Howard Spry, 19 October 1993
Jack Sullivan, 4 October 1990
Zyta Sykes, 4 June 1993
Lynette Wayling, 30 September 1993
Joy Wigglesworth, 8 October 1993
Tom Wittingslow, 6 December 1993
3RPH Radio Special, 1987
Ted Hopkins (interviewed by Merle Coppell), 23 May 1989
Ted Hopkins (interviewed by Martin Sharp & Peter Kingston), 16 July 1989

BOOKS AND JOURNAL ARTICLES

Adams, Judith A. & Edwin J. Perkins, *The American Amusement Park Industry: A History of Technology and Thrills*, Twayne Publishers, Boston, 1991.

Anderson, Norman D. & Walter R. Brown, *Ferris Wheels*, Bowling Green State University Popular Press, Bowling Green, Ohio, 1992.

Braithwaite, David & Hugh Evelyn, *Fairground Architecture: The World of Amusement Parks, Carnivals and Fairs*, Praeger, New York, 1968.

Collins, Diane, *Hollywood Down Under*, Angus & Robertson, Sydney, 1978.

Fried, Frederick, *A Pictorial History of the Carousel*, A.S. Barnes & Co. New York, 1978.

Gresham, William Lindsay, *Monster Midway*, Gollancz, London, 1954.

Jeannes, W.H., *Glenelg: Birthplace of South Australia 1855–1955*, Allen Press, Adelaide, 1955.

Jeffries, C.A., "The Greater J.D. Williams Banyan Tree" in *The Lone Hand* , 1 July 1911.

Jones, M., *North Sydney 1788–1988*, Allen & Unwin, Sydney, 1988.

Kasson, John, *Amusing the Millions: Coney Island at the Turn of the Century*, Hill & Wang, New York, 1978.

Koolhaas, Rem, *Delirious New York*, Oxford University Press, New York, 1978.

Kyriazi, Gary, *The Great American Amusement Park: A Pictorial History*, Citadel Press, Secaucus, New Jersey, 1976.

Longmire, Anne, *St Kilda: The Show Goes On: The History of St Kilda Volume 3, 1930–1983*, Hudson Publishing, Hawthorn, Victoria, 1989.

McCullough, Edo, *Good Old Coney Island*, Scribner, New York, 1957.

Mangels, William F., *The Outdoor Amusement Industry from Earliest Times to the Present*, Vantage Press, New York, 1952.

Mann, G.V.F., *The Municipality of North Sydney: History and Progress from the Earliest Settlement 1788-1938*, Municipality of the Council of North Sydney, North Sydney, 1938.

Pilat, Oliver & Jo Ranson, *Sodom by the Sea*, Garden City Publishing Co., Garden City, New York, 1941.

Rydell, Robert W., *All the World's a Fair: Visions of Empire at American International Expositions 1876–1916*, University of Chicago Press, Chicago, 1984.

Snow, Robert E. & David E. Wright, *Coney Island: A Case Study in Popular Culture and Technical Change*, Brightwaters Press, New York, 1984.

Thorne, L.G., *A History Of North Shore Sydney 1778 to Today*, Angus & Robertson, Sydney, 1966.

Weedon, Geoff & Richard Ward, *Fairground Art*, White Mouse Editions, London, 1981.

— *A Souvenir of Luna Park St Kilda – The Mecca of the Merrymaker*

— *Historic Glenelg: Birthplace of South Australia 1855–1979*, South Australia City Council.

— *St Kilda by the Sea.*

UNPUBLISHED MATERIAL

Bennett, Marsha, *A Profile of an Amusement Park: Luna Park Limited, St Kilda, Melbourne*, unpublished manuscript.

Burleigh, P.R. & R. Baker, *Luna Park, Palais Pictures & Palais de Danse*, unpublished thesis, Melbourne University Faculty of Architecture, 1965.

Friends of Luna Park, *Report on Luna Park*, unpublished, 1980.

Hopkins, E.A., *A Few Brief Facts about the History of Luna Park from its Inception until 1970*, unpublished manuscript.

Marshall, Sam, *Luna Park: Just for Fun*, unpublished thesis, University of New South Wales, Faculty of Architecture, 1982.

Matthews, Carol, *The Contribution of the Palais Theatre, St Kilda, to the Cultural Life of Melbourne*, unpublished thesis, Master of Education, Media Centre, School of Education, La Trobe University, 1985.

Reading, Graeme, *An Historical Record of the Luna Park Site Milsons Point Lavender Bay*, unpublished document, 1976.

NEWSPAPERS AND JOURNALS

Advertiser
Age
Amusement Park Journal
Argus
Australian
Australian Financial Review
Bulletin
Daily Mirror
Daily Telegraph
Daily Telegraph Mirror
Everyone's
Good Weekend
Great Northern Newspaper
Herald (Melbourne)
Herald Sun (Melbourne)
New York Times
Mosman Daily
North Shore Times
Northern Herald
Prahan Telegraph
Punch (Melbourne)
Sun (Sydney)
Sunday Herald (Melbourne)
Sunday Telegraph
Sydney Morning Herald
Tabletalk
The Lone Hand
The Sun (Melbourne)
Time
Truth (Melbourne)
Truth (Sydney)

INDEX

Photographic references are in *italics*